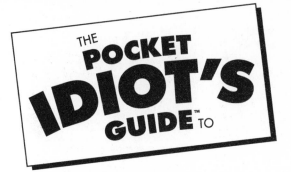

THE
POCKET
IDIOT'S
GUIDE™ TO

# Wedding Etiquette

*by Robyn S. Passante*

W9-CLF-355

**ALPHA**

A member of Penguin Group (USA) Inc.

*Dedicated to my parents, who taught me manners. And to Kostyn, to whom I will pass down those lessons.*

## ALPHA BOOKS

Published by the Penguin Group

Penguin Group (USA) Inc., 375 Hudson Street, New York, New York 10014, USA

Penguin Group (Canada), 90 Eglinton Avenue East, Suite 700, Toronto, Ontario M4P 2Y3, Canada (a division of Pearson Penguin Canada Inc.)

Penguin Books Ltd., 80 Strand, London WC2R 0RL, England

Penguin Ireland, 25 St. Stephen's Green, Dublin 2, Ireland (a division of Penguin Books Ltd.)

Penguin Group (Australia), 250 Camberwell Road, Camberwell, Victoria 3124, Australia (a division of Pearson Australia Group Pty. Ltd.)

Penguin Books India Pvt. Ltd., 11 Community Centre, Panchsheel Park, New Delhi—110 017, India

Penguin Group (NZ), 67 Apollo Drive, Rosedale, North Shore, Auckland 1311, New Zealand (a division of Pearson New Zealand Ltd.)

Penguin Books (South Africa) (Pty.) Ltd., 24 Sturdee Avenue, Rosebank, Johannesburg 2196, South Africa

Penguin Books Ltd., Registered Offices: 80 Strand, London WC2R 0RL, England

International Standard Book Number: 978-1-59257-763-7
Library of Congress Catalog Card Number: 2007941488

10  09  08      8  7  6  5  4  3  2  1

Interpretation of the printing code: The rightmost number of the first series of numbers is the year of the book's printing; the rightmost number of the second series of numbers is the number of the book's printing. For example, a printing code of 08-1 shows that the first printing occurred in 2008.

*Printed in the United States of America*

**Note:** This publication contains the opinions and ideas of its author. It is intended to provide helpful and informative material on the subject matter covered. It is sold with the understanding that the author and publisher are not engaged in rendering professional services in the book. If the reader requires personal assistance or advice, a competent professional should be consulted.

The author and publisher specifically disclaim any responsibility for any liability, loss, or risk, personal or otherwise, which is incurred as a consequence, directly or indirectly, of the use and application of any of the contents of this book.

Most Alpha books are available at special quantity discounts for bulk purchases for sales promotions, premiums, fund-raising, or educational use. Special books, or book excerpts, can also be created to fit specific needs.

For details, write: Special Markets, Alpha Books, 375 Hudson Street, New York, NY 10014.

# Contents

# Introduction

Congratulations, you're engaged! You're about to embark on one of the most exciting and harrowing journeys—planning your wedding. It's a joyous time filled with cake tastings and gown fittings. But it also can be a time of disagreements and hurt feelings if you don't follow proper etiquette rules!

This book is designed to give you a leg up on today's wedding-etiquette guidelines. Regardless of how formal or traditional your nuptials will be, you must be aware of some tried-and-true rules to ensure that your guests all feel welcome and comfortable.

I let you know what's appropriate—and what's not!—every step of the way, from wording the invitations to registering for gifts. When things have changed over time, I point out what used to be considered proper so you have a benchmark to go by. And I describe how couples of different backgrounds and circumstances handled various etiquette obstacles while planning their own nuptials.

You can have the wedding of your dreams that pleases not just you and your mate but everyone in attendance. It just takes some careful consideration and, at times, a tough decision or compromise. But don't fret: all that extra effort adds up to one wonderful wedding.

## Extras

Throughout the book, these sidebars contain extra nuggets of etiquette information:

### Wedded Bliss

Use these tips when planning your wedding to ensure proper etiquette.

### Bridal Blunder

These warning sidebars help you avoid common planning mistakes.

### History of Love

These tidbits give you background on matrimony traditions.

## Acknowledgments

I'd like to thank the brides and grooms who shared their wedding woes and etiquette missteps with me, and to the etiquette experts out there who are taxed with keeping us all in line.

Researching for this book brought back memories of planning my own wedding, and all the stress, joy, and confusion that went with it. Thanks to my mother, sisters Lisa and Kielynn-Marie, and my bridesmaids Sheila and Kim for gently guiding me in the right direction more than a few times, supporting my decisions, and rejoicing in my good fortune every step of the way.

I couldn't have done this project without my agent, Kim Lionetti at BookEnds, and the hard-working staff at Alpha Books, including Executive Editor Randy Ladenheim-Gil and Senior Development Editor Christy Wagner.

Finally and most important, thanks to God for blessings large and small. And to the two men in my life: my husband, Christopher, whose support and generosity amaze me every day, and my son, Kostyn, the light of my life. I wrote this book, in more ways than one, for you.

## Trademarks

# First Comes Money, Then Comes Marriage

## In This Chapter

- Who pays for what?
- Setting a budget
- Creating a guest list

You're engaged! Congratulations! But before you start making any plans, you must figure out how much you've got to spend on this special occasion.

In this chapter, I outline who traditionally pays for what and share the best ways to go about finding out who, if anyone, plans to help you finance your wedding. I also help you create a guest list that works for your budget.

## Wedding Finance 101

Traditionally, the bride's parents footed the bill for the wedding and reception, or at least the majority of the wedding expenses. Today, although many parents still finance their children's weddings, they're not obligated to so.

**Bridal Blunder**

Don't obligate yourself to invite someone who otherwise might not have made the cut. When speaking to potential guests, answer something non-committal, like "I'm so touched you want to come! I'm not sure yet how small or large the wedding will be, so I'll have to let you know."

Don't take for granted that either set of parents can foot the bill for whatever lavish affair you're envisioning. It's essential to have frank discussions with everyone involved early on in the planning stages so everyone is clear about who is paying for what.

## Traditionally, Who Pays for What?

When considering expenses, it's helpful to see the customary guidelines for paying wedding costs.

*Paid for by the bride:*

- Groom's ring
- Gift for the groom
- Gifts for attendants
- Blood test for marriage license

- Lodging for bride's out-of-town attendants
- Accommodations for clergy, if necessary

*Paid for by the bride's family:*

- Bridal consultant/wedding planner
- Invitations and announcements
- Church and reception flowers
- Bride's bouquet
- Bridesmaids' bouquets
- Music for ceremony, including organist fee
- Transportation of bridal party to ceremony site and reception
- Church fee
- Reception dinner
- Music at reception

*Paid for by the groom:*

- Bride's ring
- Gift for the bride
- Gifts for attendants
- Marriage license
- Mothers' corsages and boutonnieres for men in wedding party
- Lodging for out-of-town best man and ushers
- Clergyman fee
- Honeymoon expenses

*Paid for by the groom's family:*

- Traveling expenses and lodging, if necessary
- Reception beverages
- Reception hors d'oeuvres
- Gift for couple
- Rehearsal dinner

*Paid for by the bridesmaids:*

- Dress and accessories
- Transportation to and from the wedding
- Gift for couple
- Bridal shower

*Paid for by the ushers:*

- Transportation to and from the wedding
- Wedding attire rental
- Gift for couple
- Bachelor party

*Paid for by the out-of-town guests:*

- Transportation and accommodations
- Gift for couple

For years, it was standard procedure for wedding expenses to be divvied up in this manner. But these days, no hard-and-fast rules govern who should pay for what. Plenty of exceptions apply, based on the financial means of the bride, groom, their parents, and the attendants. And many couples today can pay for their own weddings. Also, attendants often pay for their own accommodations.

But there's a right way and a wrong way to figure out who should foot the bill for what. Don't automatically expect anyone to contribute or assume how much they'll give. Sit down and discuss with all parents the kind of ceremony and reception you'd like. If they're prepared to contribute to the festivities, they'll offer to do so during this conversation. It's bad form to *ask* for money for your wedding.

### Wedded Bliss

> Before you sit down with your parents to discuss money matters, talk to wedding planners about the average cost of weddings in your area, or find out the fees for the banquet hall where you'd like to hold your reception.

## The Bride's Family's Contributions

At one time, wedding receptions were almost always paid for and hosted by the bride's family. The style and formality of the party matched the bride's family's means, not the groom she was marrying. But today, there's no strict rule about the bride's family footing the bill, although many still pay for the majority of the wedding expenses.

The bride's family should not be *expected* to pay for anything, but they should be given the opportunity to contribute. The bride's family should be spoken to first about the dreams you have and plans you'd like to make. They have "first refusal" to host the affair. It's not appropriate for them to ask the groom's family to contribute. That ball rests squarely in the groom's family's court.

## The Groom's Family's Contributions

The groom's family can offer to help with the wedding expenses, although they're also not obligated to do so. If they'd like to contribute to the event, they should speak with their son and future daughter-in-law, not the bride's family. If they contribute quite a bit toward your special day, their names should appear on the invitations as co-hosts of the wedding.

## Divorced Parents' Contributions

If your parents are divorced, you should give all the parental units the courtesy of telling them your plans so they're kept in the loop and have the chance to contribute if they want. Do this separately if possible, unless your divorced parents are extraordinarily close or they had a preexisting plan to help you finance your wedding. Again, contributing anything is their choice, not their obligation.

## Financial Do's and Don'ts

As a matter of taste, don't mention what anyone else is giving you. If a question is posed, answer with a percentage of the total budget, not a figure. "Dad said he'd pay for 30 percent of the wedding costs" is more gracious than saying "Dad gave us $6,000."

Do take any gift of money offered with appreciation. Remember, some parents dream of the day they'll see their daughter or son marry, and many have saved over the years just for this occasion.

### Bridal Blunder

If you have set ideas about how you want your wedding to be and who you want to be there, don't expect a blank check from anyone without them wanting a say in your wedding, which has now become partly their party, too.

## Too Many Cooks ...

When you approach your parents about your wedding plans to discuss money, the conversation will naturally lead to ideas about the details and offers to help with planning. Be cautious about welcoming everyone's help unconditionally. You no doubt have some definite ideas about your big day, and you don't want to find yourself turning down tons of ideas from others in the months to come.

Having said that, planning a wedding ceremony and reception is quite a project, and the more help you have, the better. Married women (moms, aunts, sisters) in particular have a knack for thinking of small yet important details that brides and grooms, who are largely focused on the big-picture items, might otherwise miss.

## Help from Your Parents

You're not the only one who has dreamt about your wedding day. Your parents, especially your mother, have probably daydreamed about this day as well. They may have ideas about where it should be held, who should officiate, or what kind of meal should be served.

If your parents are footing the bill for the festivities, you should accept their ideas and incorporate them whenever possible, as they are hosting the event. However, the decisions are ultimately yours to make.

If your parents are funding the wedding and you find several sticking points between their ideas and yours, you might be wise to consider scaling down your wedding dreams and financing the event yourself.

## Help from the Wedding Planner

Wedding planners can be particularly useful when you're unfamiliar with the area where you're getting married, or when you and your parents have different ideas about the wedding. A wedding planner can serve as an impartial third party to steer you in the direction that makes the most sense for your budget and your personality.

Ask married friends in your area to recommend a wedding planner they used and liked. But as with everyone else's advice, the wedding planner is there to assist you and carry out your wishes. You have the ultimate decision-making power on most details, both large and small.

## Other Offers of Help

Be cautious when accepting help or services from friends and family. Although this can be a great money saver, it can cause friction when things don't go as you had expected.

If a family member or friend offers his or her professional services for your wedding, insist on a contract so both parties know what to expect and get what they deserve.

It's also okay to use the creative talents of loved ones for smaller things like making favors or addressing invitations. Just be sure you have a strong verbal agreement about what will be done, and set a deadline.

### Wedded Bliss

Don't skimp on the tip, when applicable, when your friends or family perform a service for you at your wedding or reception. Or give them a small gift to say thanks.

# Setting a Budget

Once you know what money, if any, parents or other loved ones will contribute, you should decide how much you can comfortably afford to spend on your nuptials. It's imperative that you set your wedding budget and stick to it if you don't want to start your marriage in debt.

### Bridal Blunder

Weddings bring out generosity in people. But just because Aunt Sandy gave your sister $1,000 for her wedding, don't count on her doing the same for you.

The trick to having a happy wedding day without breaking the bank is to make your wedding dreams fit your budget, not the other way around. Just about every wedding detail can be scaled up or down to fit your wallet. It just takes a little planning and imagination.

## Your Favorite Things

So you have a magic number—the amount you can afford to spend on your wedding. Now you have to stretch that number to pay for a million details, large and small.

It seems like an impossible task, but it's doable if you're willing to compromise. Sit down with your betrothed and pick a few things that are most important to you. You might have a certain banquet hall in mind, or maybe you always envisioned dancing to a live jazz band at your reception. Whatever you decide together is most important, that's where you should spend more money to get what you want.

In doing so, be prepared to modify your dreams on a few other details to save money and still get the wedding you always wanted.

## The Devil's in the Details

When taking a look at your budget, be sure to save some cash for tips, last-minute expenses, contract deposits, and other details. And keep track of *every dime*. Wedding money has a way of disappearing quickly—months before the big day.

### Wedded Bliss

Once your budget is set, open a bank account just for wedding expenses. Check the balance at the beginning of each month.

## The Guest List

You must know up-front how many guests you want at your wedding. This will depend on the type of ceremony you'd like, the ceremony and reception site you have your eye on, and how many people you can afford to feed and entertain.

## Equal Opportunities

Creating a guest list is a tricky endeavor, one of balance and compromise. Traditionally, there are three initial guest lists:

- The bride and groom's list
- The bride's parents' list
- The groom's parents' list

The bride and groom's list should comprise about 40 percent of the total number of guests. Each set of parents should invite about 30 percent of the total guests. When combined, these lists form the perfect guest list. But this is not a perfect world.

If the bride and groom are from the same area, and that is where the wedding will take place, the guest list will probably reflect both sides of the family equally. This isn't possible when the wedding is held near one family but far from the other, or when one family is much larger than the other.

It's good manners to ask all parents involved—not just those paying for the wedding—if they have any special guests they'd like to invite. If the bride's parents are paying for the reception, it's their duty to contact the groom's parents and tell them how many people they are welcome to invite. They should get this figure after talking with you about how large you want the guest list to be.

If the groom's family thinks they need more seats, they should offer to pay for the extras. This should all be coordinated between the two families and you, keeping in mind that it's not always possible to add more people if you've selected a reception site that only accommodates a limited number.

## The Numbers Game

A sure way to court disaster is to ask your parents for a list of everyone they'd like to invite. Instead, give them a ballpark number to shoot for based on how many total guests you'd like to attend. For instance, if you're planning a reception for 100, tell each set of parents to come up with 30 people they'd like to invite.

Wait until you receive the proposed guest lists from both sets of parents before creating yours. You don't want to duplicate close family friends, cousins, or neighborhood pals your mom might have already included.

And don't be greedy, either. If you find yourself with an extra 10 seats to fill, don't delve into your list of business acquaintances and casual friends until after you talk to your parents. They might have been forced to leave out someone dear to them in the interest of respecting the total number of guests you gave them permission to invite.

## Circles of Friends

Eliminating people from a guest list is excruciatingly difficult. It's hard to rank those you love.

The easiest way to avoid this is to select the initial guest list using a four-step method:

1. List immediate family and their spouses first.

2. Add your close friends.

3. Add extended family members.

4. If you have more spots available, add casual friends and business associates.

Be sure your parents add guests using this formula as well, and you'll be guaranteed to have the people who mean the most to you and your family at your nuptials.

### Wedded Bliss

The wedding guest list tends to magically grow during the planning process. To be safe, create an initial guest list that leaves you with a little wiggle room for adding more seats at the ceremony or additional tables at the banquet hall.

## To Invite Children or Not?

The decision to invite children to the reception is completely up to you. Some brides and grooms want an adults-only reception but think it's okay to make a few exceptions—say, for their sibling's children. But decisions like this leave other wedding guests who are parents—those who heeded the directive for "no kids" and hired a babysitter for their little ones—feeling resentful. Follow etiquette. Either invite all children or invite no children, but don't invite *some* children.

If you want an adults-only reception but are getting flack for it from loved ones who have children, consider inviting the kids to a small separate party. That's what Chris and Suzzane did when they got married. They wanted an adults-only reception but had relatives with children coming from out of town. Not wanting to leave out the kids, the couple hired a babysitter and invited all the children from out of town up to their bridal suite for a pizza party during the reception, which was held at the same hotel. Their parents were able to check on their kids throughout the night, and the pizza and movies were a lot more fun for the kids than the adults-oriented party downstairs.

### Wedded Bliss

When planning an adults-only reception, be mindful of out-of-town guests who might be traveling with children. Check with your friends or neighbors for names and numbers of a few babysitters. If possible, coordinate with out-of-town parents so one or two babysitters can watch all the kids that night. Paying the sitters' fees would be a nice gesture, too.

If you wish to have an adults-only reception, you must spread the word early and often. Be sure people know even before invitations go out that children are not invited. Also, it's poor etiquette to write "Adults only" or "No children" on your invitations. Instead, simply include only the names of those invited on the envelope. (For more on invitation etiquette, see Chapter 4.)

## Definite No-Shows

Resist the temptation to invite Aunt Edna from Alaska and others you are reasonably sure won't attend. Invitations sent to people who clearly can't come make you look like you're merely hoping for gifts.

If you feel, however, that not inviting dear Aunt Edna will hurt her feelings, send an invitation along with a note saying how you know she can't travel and you don't expect a gift, but you wanted to include her in the family's plans and will think of her on your big day.

## How Significant?

When trying to pare down the guest list, it's tempting to invite only your friends and not their dates, especially if they're not all that "significant."

If your friend lives with his or her significant other, both should be invited with a single invitation. If your friend has a significant other although they don't live together, both should be invited, and they each should receive their own invitation.

## Small Ceremony, Large Party

Not everyone who is invited to the reception must be invited to the ceremony. Many couples want, or need, to have a small, private ceremony and then choose to have a larger reception. This is acceptable, but communication with your guests is crucial in such cases. Send invitations for the ceremony and reception to those invited to both, and send reception-only invitations to those invited only to the reception.

**History of Love**

Everyone who is invited to the ceremony should be invited to the reception, with one exception: if the ceremony is held in a church that's very large and it's an open-church ceremony (meaning the entire congregation is invited), have light refreshments afterward for all those in attendance and then have a smaller, private reception after that.

## More Than You Can Handle

It's true that not everyone on your guest list will attend. But don't be tempted to use this as an excuse to inflate your guest list in hopes that not everyone will come so you'll have room for everyone who does. Invite only those whom you truly want and expect to be there, and be sure your venue—and checkbook—can accommodate every single person you invite.

That said, it's okay to send out a secondary set of invitations after a certain number of your initial invitees have RSVP'd that they can't attend. However, sending a second round of invitations to a "B list" of invitees is risky, as the initial RSVP date nears and word gets out that others received their invitations "weeks ago."

# The Big Decisions

## In This Chapter

- Deciding on formality
- Selecting a site
- Picking a menu
- Hiring professionals

Is it okay to wear formal wedding attire at a backyard wedding? Is there a distance that's too long for your guests to drive between the ceremony and reception sites? And how acceptable is the cash bar these days?

In this chapter, I explain what makes a wedding formal or informal, and what decisions you should make based on the formality of your event. And I tell you the right way to go about booking the places and people who will ultimately make your wedding day one to remember.

## Setting the Scene

How formal or informal your wedding is, is determined by a few things, including the time of day, the venue, and the bride's gown. If she wants a long beaded, embroidered gown with a cathedral train, she wants a formal wedding. If the couple wants to get married in their parents' backyard, the nuptials would most likely be semiformal at most. (For proper attire based on the event's formality, see Chapter 3.)

## Formal Weddings

Formal weddings are typically performed in a church or synagogue, usually in the evenings. The wedding party is large and the guests number more than 200. A formal reception includes a sit-down meal and often live entertainment. Engraved invitations are sent with formal responses expected.

**History of Love**

Religion often plays a part in formal weddings. Catholic and Jewish ceremonies lend themselves to formal weddings. Civil ceremonies run the gamut between very formal and informal.

## Semiformal Weddings

Semiformal weddings can be held just about anywhere, including a church, synagogue, hotel, country club, even a large home or garden. Guests typically number between 75 and 200, and either a sit-down dinner or a catered buffet is often served. Engraved invitations are sent with formal responses expected.

## Informal Weddings

Informal weddings take place in—you guessed it—
an informal setting such as a chapel, rectory,
courthouse, home, or garden. Typically the guest
list is fewer than 75 people, and an informal buffet,
sandwiches, or snacks are served. The food can
be catered or prepared by friends and relatives.
Invitations can be hand-written or telephoned to
the guests (if the guest list is under 50).

# Where to Wed

Some brides have a particular place in mind where
they want to tie the knot. Others have to search
high and low for a place that will accommodate
all their guests. It's important to select a venue for
the ceremony and reception that suits your nuptials' level of formality. The site you pick for the
ceremony should also complement the venue you
choose for the reception, if it's a different place.

## Time and Travel Considerations

You shouldn't expect guests to travel more than
30 minutes from the ceremony to the reception.
Likewise, don't allow more than an hour between
the end of the ceremony and the beginning of the
reception. If you're concerned about having enough
time for pictures with your bridal party, plan a
cocktail hour with hors d'oeurves for your guests
to enjoy while they wait for you.

## Making Accommodations

If you're inviting out-of-town guests, be sure sufficient overnight accommodations are available near the reception site. Give a few options of varying rates so your guests can pick the place that matches their budget.

**Wedded Bliss**

To ensure all your guests will have a place to stay, reserve a block of rooms at two or three nearby hotels. It's best to try to get two or three nights in the block. For a wedding of 150 to 200 guests, block 20 rooms at each of the 3 hotels.

And don't select a ceremony or reception site that doesn't accommodate every person on your guest list. You should never bank on some people not showing up.

## Visit the Venues

Whatever venues you choose, always conduct a face-to-face interview with the person in charge there. Even your childhood church will be seen in a different light when you're there to plan your wedding.

# The Flavor of Love

When it comes to wedding-reception food, just about anything goes. If you want to serve barbecue at your wedding, fire up the grill. If you'd like to order 100 lobsters for your loved ones, go full steam ahead. Just use common sense when deciding on a menu. Take into account your budget, the time of day, and the formality of your event.

## Feeding Your Guests

The type and amount of food you'll serve at your reception depends largely on the time of day you're getting married. Morning or lunchtime weddings call for a brunch or lunch menu, which could include anything from a waffle bar and fresh fruit to sandwiches and salads.

Early afternoon receptions usually call for something you'd serve at a tea; petit fours, tea sandwiches, and wedding cake would suffice. You don't want to serve a full meal to people who already ate lunch and have dinner plans.

Late afternoon and evening weddings are followed by a substantial meal, which could be a sit-down dinner or a buffet. Often hors d'oeuvres are served at a cocktail hour before the meal. These can be hot or cold, depending on your budget.

Buffet-style meals are considered less formal, although you can dress up a buffet with chef-attended stations. A buffet should offer a wide variety of dishes, including a few meatless dishes for vegetarians. Select dishes that hold up well for long periods of time on low heat. The entire meal may be served buffet-style, or you can opt to serve the first course seated and the main course at the buffet.

**History of Love**

These days, people are getting creative with buffets, offering several food stations scattered around the room to prevent a bottleneck of people waiting in line.

For semiformal or formal receptions, a place setting should be set at each guest's seat. At informal receptions, it's okay for the silverware to be wrapped in a napkin and picked up in the buffet line.

A buffet dinner is acceptable for informal and semiformal weddings. When serving a buffet, you must still have enough seating so that every single guest could be seated at the same time. Don't skimp on a smaller reception hall because you assume that several guests will be standing at any given time.

Very formal weddings should include a meal served at the table. Sit-down dinners can be served in a variety of ways: at *banquet style* dinners, a waiter or waitress is assigned to a table and serves and clears the dishes at that table. This style often includes a separate server who takes care of refilling drinks at that table. At *family style* dinners, food is served in dishes and platters at each table, and guests serve themselves as they would at home. At *a la russe* dinners, servers bring the food to each guest in serving dishes, and each guest helps himself.

## Raise Your Glass

The wedding toast is mandatory; using champagne for the wedding toast is not. If you're having a dry wedding or if you just don't want the expense of serving champagne to all your guests, it is acceptable to ask everyone to toast the bride and groom using whatever drink they have. Of course, you must be sure every guest has at least a glass of water and has been given the option for various sodas, teas, or juices before the toast.

The cash bar is always a matter of much debate. Couples who are trying to save money often opt to host a cash bar, or some variation of it, instead of an open bar. Traditionally, it was considered bad form to make your guests pay for anything at your wedding. They are, after all, your guests. But times are changing, and it's becoming more commonplace to have a cash bar.

An attractive way to do this is to provide beer and wine but have a stocked bar for guests who wish to pay for mixed drinks. Or you could offer "tray service," for which servers offer set drinks such as beer and wine on trays. They make their rounds at set times throughout the night, stopping in time for guests to sober up before the party ends.

### History of Love

Alcohol can be served any time of day.

Although weddings are joyous occasions that seem to call for a little alcohol, it's imperative that you provide plenty of nonalcoholic options as well.

## Let Them Eat Cake!

The wedding cake is a delicious wedding tradition. Even couples who have the most informal ceremonies still often serve some type of wedding cake to their guests. The flavors you choose for the cake and filling are up to you, but you should keep your guests in mind and not select a combination that only suits *your* tastes.

### Wedded Bliss

If you'd like a special cake flavor you don't think will have mainstream appeal, have the top layer made in your favorite flavor and opt for a more crowd-pleasing flavor for the lower tiers.

Some couples opt to save money by ordering a small decorative cake for the ceremonial cake cutting but then slice and serve a much more economical sheet cake to their guests. This is a fine cost-cutting measure, but don't cut the sheet cake in front of your guests. And be sure the decorative cake is out of sight when the slices of sheet cake begin arriving.

You don't have to offer another type of dessert besides wedding cake, but it's okay to do so.

Who doesn't love dessert choices! Be sure coffee and tea (and water refills) are available when dessert is served.

# Say It with Flowers

Wedding flowers can be simple or elaborate; either way, they add to the elegance of the affair. Just about anything goes when it comes to floral arrangements and bouquets for weddings.

## The Best Bouquets

The trick to creating the best bouquets for your wedding is to be mindful of the type of wedding, gown, and venue the flowers will be complementing. A simple, informal wedding calls for something simple, like a loose bouquet of wildflowers or a single rose. A formal wedding in a grand cathedral calls for a larger, more elaborate bouquet. The most formal ceremonies usually find the bride carrying a bouquet of all-white flowers, although this isn't a hard-and-fast rule.

**History of Love**

Long ago, bridesmaids carried pungent herbs, not flowers, to keep evil spirits away from the happy couple.

Don't order bouquets and other floral arrangements until the bride has chosen her gown and the bridesmaids' gowns. The florist will need to know the dress styles, colors, and even fabrics to help you pick the best arrangements. The bridesmaids' bouquets may match the bride's bouquet in style, but they should be smaller and at least slightly different.

Trust the florist or floral designer to tell you which flowers look good together, what will be in season when you're getting married, and whether the blooms you like will hold up in the season in which you're getting married.

For formal and semiformal weddings, order corsages for the mothers and anyone you'd like to highlight as a special part of the ceremony such as a reader or soloist. Boutonnieres are needed for the groom, ushers, fathers, and often grandfathers.

### Wedded Bliss

Give your mothers and grandmothers special recognition by ordering corsages or single roses just for them.

It's perfectly acceptable to use silk flowers in lieu of real ones. This is a big money-saver, and these days, some silk flowers and greenery look and feel very real.

## Floral Decorations

Check with the clergy at the church or synagogue, if you're getting married in such a place, to find out whether it's okay to bring in your own floral arrangements, and if so, what kind. It's good manners to donate at least one of your arrangements to the church or synagogue to decorate the altar as a thank you for use of the facility.

Also ask whether the flower girl can use real flower petals. Many facilities prohibit this tradition because of cleanup issues. Whether you're planning to throw rice or birdseed, blow bubbles or release doves, check with the wedding facility about what's acceptable and what's prohibited.

For the reception, you'll need to know how many tables you'll be decorating before placing an order for centerpiece arrangements. Remember to count the guest-book table, cake table, head table, and any other area you'll want to dress up.

Of course, fresh flowers are not the only decorations you can use. Candles, pine cones, sea shells, even fresh fruit can be artfully arranged to make beautiful centerpieces.

# A Picture's Worth a Thousand Words

Your wedding will be one of the most important days in your life, so it's natural that you'll want to remember it with photos, videos, or both.

Photographers and videographers should have a contract for you to review. Be sure to go over it with a fine-tooth comb before signing on the dotted line. Communication is key here; be clear about exactly what you want and don't want them to do, well before your wedding day.

Pick these professionals based on their body of work and their personalities. Be sure you click with them, because they'll be with you from morning 'til night on what could be the most stressful day of your life. The last thing you want is to spend the entire day shadowed by someone with a camera whose sense of humor gets on your nerves.

Remember to feed the photographer and the videographer. It doesn't have to be the same $70 meal you're serving your guests, but you should offer them some nourishment. And get a head count beforehand of any assistants they'll be bringing to help them so you will have enough food for everyone.

## Snapshot Savvy

A formal bridal portrait used to be the norm, but today many brides skip this sitting and wait until after the wedding to send a photo of both bride and groom to the local newspaper. Be sure to check with your local newspaper to find out whether they print the portrait in color or black and white.

It's okay to take photos before the wedding, although it's still considered bad luck for the bride and groom to see each other on their wedding day prior to the wedding.

To save time later, have the photographer take pictures of the bride and her parents, and the bride and her bridesmaids, before the wedding. If there's time, the photographer may be able to pull double duty and snap similar photos of the groom's side.

This way, you'll have fewer formal portraits to take after the ceremony, when everyone is eager to get to the reception.

The photographer can stand at the back of the church and take pictures of the wedding party entering and leaving the sanctuary, but there should be no photographs—certainly no flash photography—during the ceremony. Exchanging your vows is, after all, a sacred event, one you'll remember because it is an incredibly important moment, not because you have a snapshot of it.

Regardless of who pays for the photographer, consult both sets of parents before a photo order is placed to find out what prints, if any, they would like. Depending on how many pictures they want, the parents should offer to pay for their prints if they don't come with the package you're getting. You can give them the photographer's price list when you show them the proofs.

## Roll Camera!

Videographers capture what still photography can't. Every word uttered in your ceremony can be caught on tape for you to replay on every anniversary.

Also, check with the clergy or manager at the ceremony site to be sure videotaping the service is allowed. Rules might be in place about what kind of lighting and how many cameras are allowed.

**Bridal Blunder**

Be sure you're aware of what the videographer has in mind for video-taping your big day. Some brides and grooms are taken off-guard by how up-close and personal a videographer and his lights get.

## Amateur Night

These days it seems everyone has a digital camera or camera phone, and they'll all be snapping photos at your wedding. Many brides and grooms also place disposable cameras on the tables at the reception so each table's guests can snap some candid photos of each other and the party. Be sure to tell your guests from the start that you would like those cameras back at the end of the night!

People expect to be able to take photos at your wedding, and they should be able to. But it's your job to be sure all those amateur photographers don't get in the way of the professionals you've hired to document your big day. Keep tabs on the photographer and videographer, and be sure they're being given the space they need to get you your money's worth.

If you're worried about being too busy to notice what's going on around you, ask a trusted friend who isn't in the wedding party to keep tabs for you.

Introduce them to the photographer at the start of the day so the photographer knows she has an ally in the crowd.

# Marriage Melodies

Music is a beautiful part of the wedding ceremony and an essential part of the reception, setting the mood and serving as an elegant backdrop to your special day. When hiring professionals, be sure to get contracts signed and details discussed well before the wedding day.

Music can be a perfect way for talented loved ones to become a part of the festivities. When a loved one has offered his or her talents, discuss exactly what you'd like them to play, and for how long. Do this prior to the wedding day.

## Ceremony Music

Secular music is acceptable to play at a wedding ceremony, but you must okay it with the pastor or rabbi if you're marrying in a house of worship. Ceremony music is usually performed by an organist or pianist, but string quartet, brass ensemble, harpist, or acoustic guitarist would also be lovely.

Asking talented musician friends to perform during your ceremony is a nice way to include those you love. Be sure they're comfortable playing in front of a crowd, and be aware that if they're not professionals, they may rely on you to have acceptable outlets at your ceremony site and any necessary amplifying equipment. Remember to thank them with a gift at the rehearsal dinner.

If you hire professionals, don't wait until the rehearsal to give them the sheet music or names of songs you'd like them to play. And if you're expecting them to stick around and play during the receiving line or cocktail hour, be sure to spell that out in the contract.

## The Band Played On

Music at a reception is a must, whether it's a casual backyard barbecue or a fancy dinner/dance. Include fast and slow tunes from several generations and genres to make everyone happy and fill your dance floor.

The most formal receptions include a live band. A semiformal reception may have a band or hired DJ. The most informal parties don't have to have hired musical entertainers, but do make an effort to play some type of background music, even if it's an iPod playlist piped over your stereo speakers.

Larger bands will have you sign a "rider" that outlines what's required for the band to perform. Read this carefully and comply with it fully, if possible. If there's something in the rider you cannot do, discuss this with the band leader or booking agent prior to the wedding day. You don't want unhappy entertainers setting the mood for your party.

**Wedded Bliss**

Bands require a certain amount of space, access to electrical outlets, and other things to perform. Get a list of the band's requirements and go over them with your reception manager.

If your reception is outside, check the noise ordinance for the neighborhood. There could be certain decibel and time restrictions that need to be followed.

If your reception is during a mealtime, band members and DJs should be fed. Regardless of what time of day your reception is, offer these professionals nonalcoholic drinks and snacks, too.

## Mister DJ

A DJ also often serves as a master of ceremony, introducing the wedding party and orchestrating the first dance and cake-cutting. You can let him have as much or as little control of the evening as you wish, but you must make your requirements known early on. And give him feedback—politely—throughout the night so he can continue to meet your needs. Tell him what you want him to play!

You can give the DJ a list of songs you'd like played, but refrain from becoming an amateur DJ yourself. Let the pro do what you're paying him to do while you enjoy the evening. Also, before you give the DJ a list of favorites you want played, listen to them with a grandmother's ear and nix any that have obscene lyrics or are just not danceable.

### Wedded Bliss

Hire a DJ whose style matches your personality. A good DJ will sense the mood of the crowd before proceeding with any fun and games, but it's up to you to be sure the right person is hired to do the job.

Musicians and DJs typically wear black, but be sure to let them know how formal your reception will be and what you require them to wear.

Chapter **3**

# A Little Help from Your Friends

## In This Chapter

- The members of the wedding party
- Divvying up responsibilities
- Dressing your wedding party

Getting several people dressed appropriately and smiling sincerely on your wedding day is no small task. Selecting the right attendants and making their responsibilities clear to them are essential undertakings if you want smooth sailing up the aisle.

In this chapter, I discuss the ins and outs of selecting attendants. I tell you what duties and expenses each person in your wedding party is responsible for, and I give you the lowdown on how to outfit your best friends—and yourself—without breaking any etiquette rules.

# A Look at the Wedding Party

You probably thought about who would be in your wedding long before you were even engaged. The people selected for this honor should be relatives or close friends of the wedding couple. But as with the guest list, there needs to be a cutoff point. These are the people in your innermost circle of life, those you go to in crisis or in celebration.

## Who to Ask

It's appropriate for male siblings of the bride to be groomsmen and for female siblings of the groom to be bridesmaids. It's also appropriate for the father of the groom to be the best man, but the mother of the bride should not be matron of honor. She's considered one of the hostesses of the reception and will be busy attending to wedding guests. The mother of the bride already holds a place of honor in the front pew of the ceremony.

Also, in the past, an uneven number of attendants was discouraged but is more accepted these days. The old rule was that there could be more ushers than bridesmaids but not more bridesmaids than ushers. Today, though, that rule may be broken.

Do give special consideration to those who have asked you to be in their wedding, but don't think that just because you've been the best man in three weddings you have to return the favor on your wedding day. Be selective and then be clear to those close friends who aren't asked to be attendants that logistics prevents you from giving them that honor.

**History of Love**

Long ago, the groom would gather his strongest pals to help him kidnap his bride. His friends would then stand guard at the ceremony, ready to fend off anyone—including her family—who tried to steal her back. Those warriors of old have been replaced by today's dapper groomsmen, who almost always leave their swords at home.

Remember that your attendants hold a place of honor at your nuptials and should be treated accordingly. Bridesmaids and groomsmen should be asked to be in your wedding within a few weeks of your announcing your engagement. You should do this in person or over the phone, not by e-mail or "through the grapevine." And never assume someone already knows he or she is in the wedding party until you have a conversation with them.

Also, be mindful that accepting an invitation to be in any wedding comes with obligations of time and money. Sometimes people you love just can't swing such a commitment. Give all your attendants-to-be the time to think about whether they'd like to accept your invitation, and don't be resentful or hurt if they turn you down.

## The Maid of Honor

The maid of honor is the bride's single sister or closest single friend and has the sometimes-daunting task of supporting the bride during the wedding planning process. She may be called on to help shop for the wedding gown and to scout out places to hold the reception. She helps plan a bridal shower and coordinates other activities among the bridesmaids, including a bachelorette party if there is one and the purchase of a gift for the bride from the attendants.

On the day of the wedding, the maid of honor helps to be sure the bride is ready to go on time and is in charge of keeping the bride looking her best throughout the day, including adjusting her veil and train and touching up her makeup. She stands closest to the bride during the ceremony and holds the bride's bouquet during the exchanging of vows. She may also be asked to hold the groom's ring until the exchanging of rings. Traditionally she sits to the groom's left during the reception.

## The Matron of Honor

The matron of honor is the bride's married sister or closest married friend. There's not usually both a maid of honor and matron of honor, but it is permissible. If you have both in your wedding party, the maid of honor takes precedence, standing closest to the bride, holding the bride's bouquet and signing the marriage license as an official witness to the nuptials. The matron of honor stands between the maid of honor and the bridesmaids.

If you only have a matron of honor, she fulfills the roles a maid of honor would, including holding your bouquet, assisting you with your dress and veil, and coordinating the bridal shower and attendants' gift to the bride, if they choose to give one.

## The Best Man

The best man is typically the groom's father, brother, or best friend. He holds a title of honor, to be sure, but he has several responsibilities. He is essentially the groom's right-hand man, making sure he's dressed and ready for the ceremony on time, with his wits—and his rings—about him. The best man is the kind of guy who can be entrusted with keeping the bride's wedding ring safe until the ceremony starts.

Traditionally, the best man gives the wedding officiant his or her fee before the ceremony and is in charge of the couple's transportation from the ceremony to the reception.

The best man enters the church with the groom and stands behind him to his left. He sits to the bride's right at the reception table and gives the first toast at the reception. He also selects a gift to be given to the groom from the ushers and often coordinates bachelor party activities.

## The Bridesmaids

These are sisters, cousins, and/or close friends of the bride, and occasionally sister(s) of the groom. The number of bridesmaids corresponds with the formality of the wedding. An informal wedding should not have more than a couple bridesmaids.

Bridesmaids' duties include forming the processional at the ceremony and standing beside the bride during the nuptials. They do not, however, stand in the receiving line.

These women serve as "deputy hostesses" at the reception, mingling with guests and making sure the bride is assisted in any way she needs. The bridesmaids work with the maid or matron of honor and the bride's other friends to plan the bridal shower. They also are invited to the bachelorette party, if there is one.

Bridesmaids pay for their own dress, hair, and makeup, as well as for their own transportation to the wedding. The bride and groom are responsible for transporting their wedding party from the ceremony to the reception. Traditionally, the bride also paid for her bridesmaids' accommodations if they were coming from out of town. This is not always done today, nor is it required.

## The Groomsmen

Groomsmen, also called ushers, are usually brothers, cousins, and/or close friends of the groom, and occasionally brothers of the bride. The number of groomsmen correlates with the formality and size of the wedding.

At the wedding, groomsmen see to it that all guests are seated appropriately. They roll out the carpet for the processional and stand beside the groom during the ceremony. They escort the bridesmaids back down the aisle after the service, but they do not stand in the receiving line.

**History of Love**

A rule of thumb for ushers: you need 1 usher for every 50 wedding guests.

Groomsmen attend the bachelor party and may even help the best man plan the festivities. They pay for their own wedding clothes and contribute to a joint gift for the groom, which the best man selects.

## The Junior Bridesmaid

A junior bridesmaid is a girl between the ages of 8 and 14 who is close to the bride but too young to be a bridesmaid. Younger sisters and close cousins often fall into this category, as do children of either the bride or the groom from a previous relationship.

A junior bridesmaid walks in the processional but is not part of the receiving line. She does not help the bridesmaids plan the shower but is invited and, if possible, should attend. Her parents are responsible for paying for her dress, shoes, and hair. She and her parents should be invited to the rehearsal dinner.

## The Junior Usher

A junior usher is a boy between the ages of 10 and 14 who is close to the groom but too young to be a groomsman. Younger brothers and close cousins often fall into this category, as do children of either the bride or the groom from a previous relationship.

A junior usher is part of the wedding party merely because he is special to the bride and groom. He has very few duties other than to walk with the processional and pose for formal pictures with the rest of the wedding party. His parents are responsible for paying for his wedding clothes. He and his parents should be invited to the rehearsal dinner.

## The Flower Girl

The flower girl is typically a relative of the bride between 3 and 7 years old. She walks before or sometimes with the ring bearer during the processional, carrying a small bouquet or a basket of rose petals.

The flower girl is not a mandatory part of the bridal party. She's there because she's special to the bride and groom. She has very few duties other than to walk with the processional and pose for formal pictures with the rest of the wedding party. Her parents are responsible for paying for her dress and shoes. She and her parents should be invited to the rehearsal dinner.

**Wedded Bliss**

If you're going to have your flower girl sprinkle rose petals up the aisle, consider having her use silk petals instead of real ones. Fake petals keep their color and shape and are easier to clean up. Sites that don't allow real petals might be okay with fake ones, but do ask.

## The Ring Bearer

The ring bearer is typically a relative of the bride or groom between 3 and 7 years old. He precedes the bride in the processional, often carrying the wedding ring or rings—or fake versions if you're worried they'll get lost—on a velvet or satin pillow.

The ring bearer is not a mandatory part of the bridal party. He's there because he's special to the bride and groom. He has very few duties other than to walk with the processional and pose for formal pictures with the rest of the wedding party. His parents are responsible for paying for his wedding clothes and shoes. He and his parents should be invited to the rehearsal dinner.

## Outfitting Your Party

Dressing your wedding party is one of the most fun, yet most stressful, parts of the wedding planning process. Colors, fabrics, lengths, styles—there are so many decisions to make and several missteps to avoid.

The first step is to consider how formal your wedding is going to be. Also consider the season, ceremony site (is it indoors or outdoors?), and your personality. There are rules for each person in your bridal party, which helps tremendously when trying to figure out what's appropriate.

## The Bride

These are the basic guidelines for the bride's attire based on the formality of the occasion:

- *Formal daytime:* Floor-length white dress with long train and veil, although chapel-length train is acceptable.
- *Formal evening:* Floor-length white dress, often adorned with beads, embroidery, or other ornamentation, with long train and long veil. Gloves are optional.
- *Semiformal daytime:* Long dress with a chapel, sweep, or detachable train; veil not longer than the train.
- *Semiformal evening:* Same as semiformal daytime, with additional accessories such as gloves.
- *Informal daytime:* Simple dress with no train; short or no veil.
- *Informal evening:* Simple long or short dress with no train; veil is optional.

**Wedded Bliss**

Facials, waxing, and tanning all should be done 2 or 3 days before your nuptials to give your skin time to heal and look its best.

It's okay to borrow a wedding dress, as long as you take excellent care of it. And give a gift to the person who owns the dress. A small framed portrait of you in the dress is appropriate, but you should give an additional token of your gratitude as well.

It's appropriate for a second-time bride to wear white if she wishes. However, she shouldn't wear a veil, and her dress should not have a train; these are both associated with first-time brides.

Almost as important as the dress are the shoes. Some brides opt to wear fancy heels for the ceremony and then change into something more comfortable for the reception. That's okay, but there is such a thing as "too comfortable." Reserve sneakers and flip-flops for the honeymoon. Instead, select a medium heel and be sure you walk around in them before your wedding day. And always scuff the soles of new shoes to avoid slipping on stairs and polished floors.

## The Groom

These are the basic guidelines for the groom's attire based on the formality of the occasion.

- *Formal daytime:* Dark gray or black morning coat, gray-striped trousers, waistcoat, wing-collared shirt or ascot, and black lace-up shoes.

- *Formal evening:* Full-dress tailcoat with matching trousers, white waistcoat with bow tie, and wing-collared shirt. Top hat and gloves are optional.

- *Semiformal daytime:* Club or stroller coat with striped trousers, gray four-in-hand tie, white fold-down collared shirt, and black lace-up shoes. Or the groom can wear a dark suit with dress shirt and tie.

- *Semiformal evening:* Tuxedo with matching trousers, dress shirt, bow tie or four-in-hand tie, and vest or cummerbund. Summertime weddings call for white or ivory dinner jackets.

- *Informal daytime:* Suit or blazer, dress shirt, and four-in-hand tie.

- *Informal evening:* Dark suit, dress shirt, and four-in-hand tie.

If the groom is in the armed forces, he may wear his dress uniform. If all his groomsmen also are in the military, they may wear their dress uniforms as well. However, if only some of his groomsmen are in the military, it's best for them to dress in civilian suits to match the rest of the wedding party.

In a formal wedding, the groomsmen and father of the bride should wear the same style of tuxedo or suit as the groom. The groom may be set apart from his attendants in the following ways:

- The groom wears a different color vest and tie.

- The groom wears a vest and tie in a different fabric.

- The flowers in the boutonniere worn in the groom's left lapel are a different variety and color than his groomsmen's.

- Only the groom may wear a top hat, cummerbund, or other accessory.

### Bridal Blunder

A groom should not get his hair cut the day before the wedding. Schedule an appointment for at least one week before the big day.

## The Bridesmaids

These are the basic guidelines for the bridesmaids' attire based on the formality of the occasion:

- *Formal daytime:* Long dresses in evening-wear styles, with high heels.

- *Formal evening:* Long dresses in evening-wear styles, with high heels. The dresses may be embellished with beads or sequins.

- *Semiformal daytime:* Long or short dresses that complement the bride's style of dress; high heels.

- *Semiformal evening:* Long or short dresses that complement the bride's style of dress and may have sequin or crystal embellishments; high heels.
- *Informal daytime:* A suit or dress, less elaborate than semiformal wedding; high heels or sandals.
- *Informal evening:* Cocktail-length dress or suit; high heels or sandals.

When selecting bridesmaid dresses, be mindful of your attendants' figures and ages. Consider the cost as well because they most likely will be footing the bill for their own dresses. You may take along the bridesmaids to shop for and try on dresses, but ultimately, it's the bride's decision. Some brides select a few different styles in the same fabric and color so the bridesmaids can choose the most flattering style for themselves.

Bridesmaids' shoes may be dyed to match the dresses, but they don't have to be. Many brides today choose to outfit their attendants in silver, gold, or black shoes that complement the dresses. It's okay for the bride to give a loose guideline, like "Get some silvery strappy heels," and allow her maids to find the style and height that suits them best.

Let each bridesmaid wear their hair and makeup in the style that suits them. If you want uniformity, concentrate your efforts on the jewelry and shoes your attendants will wear. It's okay to hire a hairstylist and makeup artist for the day of your wedding, but the choice to use (and, of course, pay) for their services should be left up to each bridesmaid.

The maid or matron of honor may be set apart by wearing a dress in the same style but a deeper shade than the bridesmaids. She also may carry a slightly larger bouquet than the bridesmaids, but not as big as the bride's. If there is just one attendant in the wedding, she should be dressed in a style similar to the bride, only simpler, with a smaller bouquet in complementary colors.

The bride should gather the bridesmaid measurements and order the dresses. But it's up to each bridesmaid to get the necessary alterations well before the wedding day.

## The Groomsmen

These are the basic guidelines for the groomsmen's attire based on the formality of the occasion:

- *Formal daytime:* Dark gray or black morning coat, gray-striped trousers, waistcoat, wing-collared shirt or ascot, and black lace-up shoes.
- *Formal evening:* Full-dress tailcoat with matching trousers, white waistcoat with bow tie, wing-collared shirt. Top hat and gloves are optional.
- *Semiformal daytime:* Club or stroller coat with striped trousers, gray four-in-hand tie, white fold-down collared shirt, and black

lace-up shoes. Or the groomsmen can wear a dark suit with dress shirt and tie.

- *Semiformal evening:* Tuxedo with matching trousers, dress shirt, bow tie or four-in-hand tie, and vest or cummerbund. Summertime weddings call for white or ivory dinner jackets.

- *Informal daytime:* Suit or blazer, dress shirt, and four-in-hand tie.

- *Informal evening:* Dark suit, dress shirt, and four-in-hand tie.

If the men in the wedding party are renting their formalwear, they should do so at least three months before the wedding. It's best to order the suits from the same place rather than from several different shops. The groom should take care of the details of getting his groomsmen's measurements and placing the order.

Each groomsman should try on his suit as soon as he picks it up, as adjustments often need to be made. Don't wait until the night before the wedding to find out that your pants are too short!

## The Mothers of the Bride and Groom

These are the basic guidelines for the mothers' attire based on the formality of the occasion:

- *Formal daytime:* Long or short dresses, not as formal as those for evening, in fabrics such as chiffon, lace, taffeta, crepe, or silk satin. Hats and gloves are optional.

- *Formal evening:* Long evening dresses with embellishments in colors that complement the bridesmaids' dresses and each other.

- *Semiformal daytime:* Elegant dresses or pantsuits.

- *Semiformal evening:* Long or short dresses or evening suits (not business suits).

- *Informal daytime:* Simple, elegant daytime suits or dresses.

- *Informal evening:* Short evening dresses or dinner suits.

Traditionally, the mother of the bride chooses her outfit first and then describes it to the mother of the groom so she can find something complementary. The colors of both gowns should blend with but not exactly match the colors in the wedding party. Both women may wear the same color but not the same dress. If a stepmother will be in the receiving line and in formal wedding pictures, she should adhere to these guidelines, too.

## The Fathers of the Bride and Groom

These are the basic guidelines for the fathers' attire based on the formality of the occasion.

- *Formal daytime/evening:* The father of the bride should dress the same as the groom. If the groom's father is not in the wedding party, he should dress like the rest of the wedding guests.

- *Semiformal daytime/evening:* Both fathers should dress the same as the groom, but if the father of the groom is not in the wedding party, he may wear a dark suit.
- *Informal daytime/evening:* Both fathers dress in the same style of clothes as the groom.

Although the fathers should wear the same style suit as the groomsmen, they needn't wear colored ties, cummerbunds, or vests to match the groomsmen. They should stick with basic black for these accessories. They should, however, have boutonnieres that match the groomsmen's.

If the father is a retired military officer, he may wear his dress uniform, depending on the formality of the wedding.

## The Flower Girl and Ring Bearer

Opinions are split in regard to the attire for child members of the wedding party. Some say that no matter the degree of formality, children in the wedding party should dress as children, not miniature versions of the adults. Others say that child-size tuxedoes and smaller versions of bridesmaid dresses are acceptable. It's really up to the bride and groom.

Consider the children when deciding their outfits. Very small children might not be comfortable wearing mini tuxedoes and long, scratchy dresses. For their comfort without sacrificing style, flower girls and ring bearers may wear what they would wear to a special church service.

# Your Presence Is Requested

## In This Chapter

- Mark your calendar!
- Writing and addressing wedding invitations
- Using the Internet to communicate with your guests
- Spreading the word about last-minute changes

Many people fret when it comes to sending wedding invitations. What's the proper wording? How should they be addressed? When should they be sent out?

In this chapter, I help you find the perfect wording for your invitations and walk you through the do's and don'ts of addressing the envelopes. I also discuss the use of the Internet to keep guests up to date on your wedding plans and tell you what to do for last-minute changes, postponements, or canceled weddings.

# Save the Date

Save-the-date cards are still a nice idea, especially if you're getting married during a holiday weekend or in a month that's traditionally busy for families. The cards needn't be engraved, but they should match the formality and, if possible, the color and style of the wedding invitations that will follow. Some brides and grooms have opted to send postcards or have refrigerator magnets printed with the wedding date, time, and place. Typical wording follows:

Please save the date of
Saturday, the tenth of October
two thousand and nine
for the wedding of
Miss Jane Ann Smith to Mr. John David Jones
in Saratoga Springs, New York

The card includes the names of those hosting the event with "invitation to follow" at the bottom. If you're inviting several out-of-town guests, it's a good idea to include relevant hotel information if possible so they can begin making travel plans.

Save-the-date cards don't require a response. And they are not to be used in lieu of formal invitations.

# Invitation Basics

There's something about seeing your wedding invitations fresh from the printer in neat little piles that makes this whole thing very real. Finally you recognize your wedding day as an official event: those are *your* names engraved on that shiny paper, along with the exact date and time your lives will change forever.

Getting to that point, however, is much more involved than you might think. You will no doubt pore over dozens of sample invitations. You'll discuss types of printing, font styles, wording choices, ink colors, and paper weight. Decide all those choices based on your preference and the formality of your wedding. Unless you have flawless penmanship (think professional calligrapher), your invitations should not be handwritten, although your envelopes may be.

### Wedded Bliss

Before you shop for invitations, get your details straight. Know the exact spelling of the ceremony and reception sites (both the name of the building and the town it's in), how your parents want their names to appear, if at all, and how many invitations you need. Double-check with your contacts for both the ceremony and the reception to be sure the times you've discussed are final.

Order invitations at least 6 months before the wedding. This gives you adequate time to fix errors if there are any, as well as address, assemble, and mail them. They should be sent 6 to 8 weeks before the wedding.

## Deciding on Wording

Wedding invitations are an indication to your guests about the type of wedding they're invited to, from the very formal to the very informal. It's fine to add a touch of your personalities to the invitation, but stay away from wording that's too hokey or graphics that devalue the elegance of the party you're planning. For all but the most informal wedding invitations, all words (except Mr., Mrs., Dr., and other titles) should be spelled out.

> **History of Love**
>
> Invitations to religious wedding ceremonies typically use the more formal wording "request the honour of your presence," whereas invitations to civil ceremonies are worded "request the pleasure of your company."

Traditionally, the host of the party is listed first on the invitation. The names of those betrothed follow, along with the time, date, and place of the wedding. Following are examples of the wording choices for the most common configurations of who hosts the wedding.

*When the bride's parents host:*

> Mr. and Mrs. Patrick Evans Smith
> request the honour of your presence
> at the marriage of their daughter
> Jane Ann
> to
> Mr. John David Jones
> Saturday, the tenth of October
> at five o'clock
> St. Luke's United Methodist Church
> Saratoga Springs, New York

*When the bride's father holds a title:*

> Dr. and Mrs. Patrick Evans Smith
> request the honour of your presence
> at the marriage of their daughter
> Jane Ann
> to
> Mr. John David Jones ...

*When the bride's mother holds a title:*

> Mr. Patrick Evans Smith
> and
> Dr. Marcy Hayden Smith
> request the honour of your presence
> at the marriage of their daughter
> Jane Ann ...

*When both the bride's and the groom's parents host:*

> Mr. and Mrs. Patrick Evans Smith
> and Mr. and Mrs. David Jeffrey Jones
> request the honour of your presence
> at the marriage of their children
> Miss Jane Ann Smith
> and
> Mr. John David Jones ...

*When the bride's parents host but the groom's parents
want to be listed:*

> Mr. and Mrs. Patrick Evans Smith
> request the honour of your presence
> at the marriage of their daughter
> Jane Ann
> to
> Mr. John David Jones
> son of Mr. and Mrs. David Jeffrey Jones ...

*When the bride and groom host:*

> Miss Jane Ann Smith
> and Mr. John David Jones
> request the honour of your presence
> at their marriage ...

*When the bride's mother is deceased:*

> Mr. Patrick Evans Smith
> requests the honour of your presence
> at the marriage of his daughter ...

*When the bride's father is deceased:*

> Mrs. Patrick Evans Smith
> requests the honour of your presence
> at the marriage of her daughter ...

*Or:*

> Mrs. Marcy Hayden Smith
> requests the honour of your presence
> at the marriage of her daughter ...

**Wedded Bliss**

Don't include the name of a deceased parent on a wedding invitation, but you can still honor that person on your wedding day. Light a memorial candle or display a special floral arrangement and mention its purpose in your bulletin. Or include a prayer or poem dedicated to their memory.

*When both of the bride's parents are deceased:*

> Miss Jane Ann Smith
> daughter of the late Mr. and Mrs. Patrick Evans
> Smith
> and
> Mr. John David Jones
> request the honour of your presence ...

*When the bride's parents are divorced and both are hosting:*

> Mrs. (or Ms.) Marcy Hayden Smith
> and
> Mr. Patrick Evans Smith
> request the honour of your presence
> at the marriage of their daughter
> Jane Ann
> to
> Mr. John David Jones ...

*When the bride's mother has remarried and she and her husband are hosting:*

> Mr. and Mrs. Gary Thomas Rollins
> request the honour of your presence
> at the marriage of her daughter
> Jane Ann Smith
> to
> Mr. John David Jones ...

*When the bride's father has remarried and they are hosting:*

> Mr. and Mrs. Patrick Evans Smith
> request the honour of your presence
> at the marriage of his daughter
> Jane Ann
> to
> Mr. John David Jones ...

*Not naming parents:*

> Jane Ann Smith and John David Jones
> together with their parents
> request the honour of your presence
> at their marriage ...

*When the bride and groom have children they want listed:*

> Jane Ann Smith
> and
> John David Jones
> together with their children
> Ella Ann Smith, Gregory James Smith, and
> John David Jones Jr.
> request the honour of your presence
> at their marriage ...

*When live-in partners host the wedding:*

> Mr. Daniel James Stedman
> Mr. Stephen Adam Alston
> request the honour of your presence
> at the marriage of Mr. Stedman's daughter
> Carolyn Grace
> to Christopher Mark Burton ...

*When someone other than the bride's parents host the wedding:*

> Mrs. Mary Jane Smith
> requests the honour of your presence
> at the marriage of her granddaughter
> Jane Ann
> to
> Mr. John David Jones...

## What to Include

There are many enclosures to send with the invitations, and for every piece of paper you add, more postage is needed. The basic invitation includes the following elements:

- The invitation to the wedding and reception
- A response card
- A response card envelope (preaddressed and stamped)
- Directions and maps
- Hotel information
- The inner envelope to hold all these elements, usually handwritten with the full names of the people being invited (For semiformal and informal weddings, this envelope is no longer considered necessary.)
- The outer envelope that holds everything, addressed with the guest's full name and address

**History of Love**

Today, couples almost always include a response card along with a preaddressed and stamped envelope.

If you're hosting a morning-after brunch, include an invitation card alongside the wedding invitation. These cards should be simple and indicate that the brunch guest list is limited. Use wording like "Please join the wedding party for a morning-after brunch at the Congress Street Inn at 10 A.M. Sunday, the eleventh of October" so invitees won't start chatting about the brunch to extended family or friends who aren't invited. When sending these cards, be careful to insert them in the proper envelopes!

### Wedded Bliss

When getting a final count for ordering your invitations, don't forget everyone in your wedding party, the clergy person and his or her spouse, both sets of parents, and extras for yourself to keep as mementos.

## What *Not* to Include

The wedding invitation is used to indicate the wedding's time, date, and place. This is not the opportunity for the bride and groom to offer "rules" to their wedding guests. Don't write directives such as "No smoking," "No children," or "No gifts, please" on the invitation. You can, however, include "Black tie invited" if you're having a formal wedding. This will give your guests a clue to the formality of the event and the proper dress for the day.

## Addressing Invitations

It's not good etiquette to use computer-generated address labels. Addresses should be handwritten using a professional calligrapher or a friend with excellent penmanship.

On the inner envelope, write the name of the person who is invited. It's fine to use only the couple's last name if they're married, but their full names should go on the outer envelope. For example, you may write "Mr. and Mrs. Johnson" on the inner envelope, but on the outer envelope, you would write "Mr. and Mrs. Daniel M. Johnson." Note: for the most formal weddings, the middle name is spelled out. For less-formal weddings, the middle initial may be used.

The inner envelope may bear the first names of close friends ("John and Maria") or nicknames of very close family members ("Grammy and Pop-Pops"). But the outer envelope should include their full names.

If children under 18 are invited include their names on the inner envelope but not the outer envelope. If there are too many children to name, you can write "The Smith Family," but *only* if every person in that immediate family is invited. If they have an older child who lives outside the home but is invited, he should receive his own invitation.

For an unmarried couple living at the same address, only one invitation is necessary. On the outer envelope, write the full names of both on separate lines in alphabetical order. The inner envelope should include courtesy titles with their last names only, listed on the same line (e.g., "Miss Kennedy and Mr. Stedman), also in alphabetical order.

### Bridal Blunder

Guests know whether their children are invited if the children's names are included on the invitation envelope—or pointedly left off. Still, be sure you spread the word.

The outer envelope is addressed with the invitee's full name and address, as well as your return address. Titles such as Mr., Mrs., and Dr. can be abbreviated, as can Boulevard, but all streets (Street, Road, Drive), cities, and states should be spelled out.

Roommates living at the same address should receive separate invitations. If you're allowing single friends to bring dates, find out the name of the date your friend plans to invite and include that name on your friend's invitation. It's best to avoid the generic "and guest," especially if you know your friend has a significant other who will most likely attend. It's okay not to allow for single friends to come with guests, but make that clear to them.

When addressing an invitation to a couple in which one member has a courtesy title, list that person first. For example, you would write "Dr. Simmons and Mr. Simmons" on the inner envelope. The outer envelope would look like this:

Dr. Sylvia Simmons
Mr. Martin Simmons
3013 Bay Street
Beaufort, South Carolina 29902

# World Wide Weddings

All this fuss over formal wedding invitations may seem silly to today's couples, who no doubt already have spread the word via e-mail and wedding websites about the details of their big day. A lot of etiquette rules have relaxed in recent years, but using the web to invite guests to your wedding is not one of them. Formal invitations must still be sent through the mail.

That said, the web is a great place to let people know about your wedding day plans as they develop. Wedding websites enable you to keep even the largest guest list up to speed on everything from your wedding day forecast to the entrée choices you've selected.

Bridal shower invitations also should be sent through the mail, although you may include the web address for your wedding website on the invitation. A wedding website is a good place to post registry information and an address where gifts may be shipped.

It is acceptable to send e-vites to people for bachelor and bachelorette parties.

# Hear Ye, Hear Ye

Sometimes there's no need for invitations because there's no formal wedding reception. People get married without a fuss, or very quickly, for various reasons. That doesn't mean they shouldn't herald the good news across the miles.

A typical wedding announcement, which can be printed or hand-written, includes the names of the betrothed and the date and place of the wedding. Traditionally they bear the names of the bride's parents who are "making" the announcement.

Mr. and Mrs. Patrick Evans Smith
are pleased to announce
the marriage of their daughter
Jane Ann Smith
to
Mr. John David Jones
Saturday, the fifth of May
two thousand and eight
Saratoga Springs, New York

Besides announcing a wedding that took place with little to no fanfare, wedding announcements can be used to share your news with people, such as co-workers, who you cannot afford (or don't wish) to invite to your wedding and reception. But wedding announcements are not meant to elicit gift-giving. It's not appropriate to include any sort of registry information along with your announcement.

Wedding announcements should be sent at least one day *after* the wedding. Don't tempt fate by getting ahead of yourself and mailing them before your nuptials take place. Put a bridesmaid or the mother of the bride in charge of dropping them in the mail after you've said "I do."

### Bridal Blunder

Some couples inflate their guest list with dozens of people they're sure won't attend. Such invitations are seen as pandering for a gift. Send wedding announcements instead, which carry no obligation of attendance or gift.

# Hold It Right There!

I know you're putting your heart and soul into these nuptials, but you should know something: sometimes, very rarely, things go wrong. Venues need to be changed. Weddings need to be post-poned. If this happens to you, don't panic. (I know, easy for me to say.) Take a deep breath, try to relax, and let your guests know what's up.

## Canceling the Wedding

If the wedding is canceled after the invitations have been sent, a card should be sent right away with wording similar to the following:

> Mr. and Mrs. Patrick Evans Smith
> announce that the marriage of their daughter
> Jane Ann
> to
> John David Jones
> will not take place

The cards need not be in the same style and color as the invitations themselves. If there isn't time to reach everyone by mail, a telephone call to each guest is a must.

If the wedding is canceled due to the death in the family, that detail may be given in the announcement:

> Mr. and Mrs. Patrick Evans Smith
> regret
> that the death of Mr. Jones's sister
> obliges them to recall the invitations
> to the wedding of their daughter
> Jane Ann
> to
> John David Jones
> Saturday, the tenth of October

## Postponing the Wedding

If the wedding needs to be postponed, cards should be sent out right away indicating the new date, time, and place.

Mr. and Mrs. Patrick Evans Smith
announce that the marriage of their daughter
Jane Ann
to
John David Jones
has been postponed from
Saturday, the tenth of October
until Saturday, the twenty-second of November
at five o'clock
Saint Luke's Church
Saratoga Springs, New York

Keep in mind that if the wedding has been moved *up*, you might need a new RSVP date to get an accurate head count in time to place the food order with the caterer.

If the wedding has not been postponed but has changed venues, time, or any other pertinent detail, a similar card should be sent immediately, notifying people of the change. Be sure you're clear that the note includes an important change; otherwise, people might skim over it and think *I already got an invitation to this wedding* before tossing it in the trash!

# Chapter 5

# It's Party Time!

## In This Chapter

- The rules for bridal showers
- Planning bachelor and bachelorette parties
- Getting it right with a rehearsal dinner
- Wrapping up with after-wedding parties

Weddings are huge celebrations that involve smaller celebrations in the days and weeks leading up to it. Each of these smaller parties has its own set of etiquette landmines that need to be danced around. Who should be invited? Who should be planning these shindigs? And how should you handle gifts?

In this chapter, I walk you through the basic etiquette rules of typical wedding-related parties, from the bridal shower to the bachelor party. I tell you who to invite, how to handle gift registries and party favors, and what's okay—and not okay—at bachelor and bachelorette parties.

# Showering the Bride-to-Be

The bridal shower is a time-tested tradition. A group of women of all ages gather to play silly games and eat finger sandwiches. It's also a time to shower the bride-to-be with gifts, cards, and good-humored advice. It used to be just one bridal shower per wedding, but today a bride may be the guest of honor at several showers planned by co-workers, church friends, neighbors, and relatives.

### Bridal Blunder

Some brides opt for a coed shower that includes the groom and his friends. But check with the groom first to see what kind of interest his friends, and your friends' male counterparts, have in participating. Nothing deflates a festive atmosphere quicker than when half the guests have been dragged to the party.

Bridal showers can be held anytime after the engagement announcement, but they're typically held between 2 months and 2 weeks before the wedding. They're traditionally held on Sunday afternoons, but any time and place are appropriate, as long as it's not too close to the wedding date. The bride already will have her hands—and her head—full of things she needs to get accomplished and may not have the time or the attention span for such a soirée.

## Who Plans and Pays

The bridesmaids or the bride's close friends usually plan and pay for the bridal shower, with the maid of honor playing a central role. It's considered bad form for a member of the bride or the groom's family to host a shower, because that makes it look like the family is asking for gifts for the couple.

Keep in mind that if you plan a shower during a mealtime, your guests will expect to be fed something more substantial than your average coffee, cake, and finger sandwiches.

## Who's Invited

Bridal showers should not be a surprise. There are a couple reasons for this, and a big one is that it's up to the bride to provide a guest list for the shower. But don't hand your maid of honor a list of 40 people you want invited. Instead, ask her how many people she is planning to accommodate at a shower and then tailor your guest list to this number.

Only people who will be invited to the wedding should be invited to the shower. The exception to this rule is if co-workers or other large groups of people are throwing a shower for the bride, knowing full well that they will not all be invited to the wedding. These showers should be extremely simple affairs, perhaps just a cake and a collective gift given in an office break room.

Keep in mind that your friends are going to a lot of trouble to throw you this party, so don't be disrespectful and come to them at the last minute with extra people you'd like invited. Also, be ready with phone numbers so they can call those who fail to RSVP (a common problem in shower-planning).

**Bridal Blunder**

If you're having more than one bridal shower or similar prewedding party, don't invite the same guest to more than one party unless they ask to be included.

Shower invitations can reflect the theme of the shower or the personality of the bride. If there's a theme, it should be passed through the bride for approval. It's acceptable to include the names of stores and websites where the bridal couple is registered.

## Gift-Giving and Receiving

Receiving gifts is one of the perks of getting married. A long time ago a bridal shower was given to build the bride's trousseau with the necessary items for her to make a home with her new husband. Back then, it was rare for a man and woman to live together before marriage, so they were starting from scratch when it came to kitchen appliances, bed and bath linens, and china.

Times have changed, and today many couples live together before marriage. If you and your significant

other already live together, you still can register for
necessities and traditional wedding gifts, such as
china and linens. But keep in mind that your friends
and family *know* you've been living together for
awhile and probably don't need a $300 coffee maker.

Be realistic, not greedy, when you register, and be
sure to register for several gifts with varying price
tags to accommodate every budget.

When you're registering, keep in mind that shower
gifts shouldn't be on the expensive side. Most
guests limit their spending to about $30, although
close friends and family may give more extravagant
gifts. Be sure to have plenty of gifts of this price or
less on your registry.

Many shower guests opt to save the wedding registry for wedding gifts and buy shower gifts that
aren't on the registry. It's wise for the bride to
be sure the hostess is familiar with the bride and
groom's taste when it comes to home décor. She
should know what style and colors their bedroom,
bathroom, and kitchen are done in so she might
offer gift suggestions to shower guests.

When opening shower gifts, be prepared to open
duplicate gifts. Be gracious and comment about
how two is better than one, not how much money
you'll get when you return the duplicate for something else you'd rather have. Having said that, it's
okay to exchange duplicate gifts for something else.
It's just not okay to make a show of your plans to
do so in front of the gift-givers.

**Bridal Blunder**

Be thankful and gracious for any gift you are given, whether it's on your registry or not. And never ask for money or charitable donations as shower gifts.

If you're getting married for the second time, it's generally inappropriate and unnecessary to be the guest of honor at a bridal shower. If friends insist, however, then go with the flow but consider a less showerlike coed party or barbecue.

Be sure to write the hostess, along with anyone else who helped to plan the shower, a thank you note right after the shower. A small gift of thanks also is appropriate. Thank you notes also should be promptly sent to all shower guests who brought a gift.

# One Last Hurrah with the Boys

Ah, the bachelor party. What was once a night of drunken debauchery meant to give the groom one last hurrah today is more about enjoying the camaraderie of the groom's friends, who probably don't all get together often enough. More guys today are opting for golf outings and poker night parties rather than heading to strip clubs or flying to Vegas.

One of the most important decisions is when to have the bachelor party. If you don't want the groom to show up to your wedding with a pounding headache and bags under his eyes, dissuade his pals from throwing the party the night before the wedding. It's tempting to do so, because all his groomsmen and best friends will be in the same town for the wedding. But the night before the wedding should be spent enjoying the rehearsal dinner, visiting with out-of-town relatives and friends, and getting a good night's sleep.

Hold the bachelor party at least the weekend before the wedding. If many out-of-town friends would like to attend, plan the bachelor party for some time well before the wedding so people don't have to make long-distance trips two weekends in a row.

## Who Plans and Pays

The best man usually coordinates the bachelor party activities with help from the groomsmen and guidance from the groom. Nobody should plan a particular kind of party—or the hiring of a particular kind of entertainer—without first asking the groom if this is what he'd like.

### Wedded Bliss

If your bachelor party will be an expensive affair, your best man might ask each guest, well before the party, to contribute an equal amount for the festivities. Be clear about what they're paying for, and have the best man collect and hang on to these funds for safe-keeping.

The best man may choose to foot the bill for the bulk of the party or have the groomsmen and other guests chip in. Party guests should be prepared to pay for their own food, drinks, and other expenses, depending on where the party is held.

If the party includes the consumption of alcohol, and especially if it involves moving all the partygoers from one place to another, the best man should plan for a way to get inebriated partygoers to their destination safely. This may include renting a limo or party bus or finding enough designated drivers and cars to accommodate everyone.

## Who's Invited

Every male who's in the wedding party (except those underage, if the party will include bar-hopping or other adult entertainment) should be invited. Both fathers may be invited, as well as close male friends of the groom who aren't in the wedding party. Guests do not have to be single to attend (although they obviously shouldn't show up with their spouses). Keep in mind that anyone invited to the bachelor party should also be invited to the wedding.

Formal invitations can be sent if the party is a formal event like a sit-down dinner or if it's an extravagant weekend away, for which many details need to be made clear. Invitations can be e-mailed to partygoers as well; just be sure you know everyone's e-mail address and don't allow the invitation to be forwarded to others, unless you're okay with your bachelor party becoming a free-for-all.

## Gift-Giving and Receiving

Bachelor party invitations don't come with an obligation to buy a gift. Sometimes groomsmen choose to go in on a gift for the groom, and the bachelor party is an appropriate place to present this gift to their pal.

# Anything He Can Do, I Can Do Better

Today many brides opt to have bachelorette parties, which can include anything from a day at the spa to a night on the town with her closest girlfriends. The rules of etiquette are virtually the same for both.

## Who Plans and Pays

The bride's honor attendants often pool their resources and ideas to plan the bachelorette party. It can take place at a friend's home, a fancy restaurant, a day spa, or another venue. This party doesn't have the formality of a bridal shower, but something should be planned beyond gathering at someone's house. This can be as simple as sharing a meal together or having a movie-and-makeup night with just the gals.

As with the bachelor party, invited guests should be apprised of the cost of attending the party and, when possible, funds should be collected beforehand to make things simple. Each guest should pay for her own expenses. The bride's expenses are shared equally by her bridesmaids, although the maid of honor may choose to pay for her best friend.

Like the bachelor party, if the bachelorette party will include alcohol, the hostess needs to be sure enough designated drivers are available to get all partygoers from place to place safely.

### Wedded Bliss

To avoid feelings of insecurity or jealousy regarding bachelor and bachelorette parties, plan two separate events for the same night and have both parties meet up toward the end of the night for a co-ed celebration and a big toast to both bride and groom. You finish the night the way you're going to finish every night after you're married—together.

## Who's Invited

All the bride's honor attendants should be invited (although not the junior bridesmaid or flower girl), along with any close friends or co-workers she wants to include. Guests do not have to be single to attend (although they obviously shouldn't show up with their spouses). Keep in mind that anyone invited to the bachelorette party should also be invited to the wedding.

Mothers of the bride and groom and other older relatives may be invited depending on the type of party you're planning. Be sure they understand all the activities that will take place, so they can judge whether they'll feel comfortable or not. Remember, there will be bridal showers, luncheons, and a rehearsal dinner to include them in, so don't feel bad if you'd rather keep your bachelorette party guest list to friends your own age.

Invitations can be mailed or sent via e-mail, although be careful that an e-mailed invitation doesn't get forwarded to others outside your close circle of friends whom you might not want invited.

## Gift-Giving and Receiving

Guests invited to a bachelorette party are under no obligation to bring a gift. Sometimes the honor attendants will go in on a collective gift for the bride, which may be anything from a spa gift certificate to lingerie. But they are not obligated to do so.

It is courteous for the bride to send thank you notes to those who planned the party.

# Practice Makes Perfect

As with all wedding-related parties, the rehearsal dinner can be as large or small, as formal or informal, as you want. Its degree of formality generally depends on how formal your wedding will be the following day. But that isn't always the case, because the wedding and the rehearsal dinner often are paid for by two different families who may have very different budgets.

## Who Plans and Pays

Traditionally, the groom's parents host the rehearsal dinner, although really anyone can have this honor—including the bride and groom. Whoever hosts the meal pays for it. Rehearsal dinner guests should never be asked to pay for their meal or drinks.

The rehearsal dinner should in no way upstage the following day's wedding reception. The reception menu should be selected first and given to the rehearsal dinner hosts so they don't duplicate anything. In the same way, the dinner should not be held at the ceremony or reception site, although it should be located reasonably close to the ceremony site because everyone will be coming from there after the rehearsal.

## Who's Invited

The rehearsal dinner used to be an intimate meal for those in the wedding party and both sets of parents. But these days many people feel obligated to invite other relatives of both the bride and groom as well as wedding guests who are traveling from out of town. This can make the guest list quickly add up.

Before you begin spreading the word to all your out-of-town friends about when and where the dinner will be, consult the rehearsal dinner hosts to find out how many people they're prepared to serve. If their number is far less than the number of people you feel should be invited, you'll have to pitch in to help cover the added costs. You'll also need to be sure the restaurant or dinner site the hosts have picked will accommodate the added guests.

**Wedded Bliss**

If you have several out-of-town guests coming to your wedding and can't (or don't want to) invite them all to the rehearsal dinner but want to make them feel welcome, host a small reception for those guests after the rehearsal dinner back at the hotel where most of them are staying. Invite these travel-weary guests to your hotel suite for coffee and sweets to let them know you appreciate the effort and time they've put into attending your nuptials.

If you're sticking with the basics, the following people should be invited:

- The bride's and groom's attendants, along with their spouses if they're married and are traveling from out of town
- The parents (and stepparents) of both the bride and groom
- The ring bearer and flower girl and their parents
- The officiant and his/her spouse
- The bride's and groom's immediate families (siblings and their spouses)
- The bride and groom (of course!)

If anyone has been asked to do a reading or solo during the ceremony, they (and their spouse) may be invited as well. You don't want someone who is at the rehearsal left out of the ensuing rehearsal dinner festivities.

Written invitations are optional to the rehearsal dinner, although it's a good idea, especially if the guest list is long or directions are needed. Invitations should go out five weeks before the rehearsal, and RSVPs should be directed to the host. For very casual or small rehearsal dinners, it's fine to invite people by phone or e-mail.

> **Wedded Bliss**
>
> Invite people to your rehearsal dinner one at a time so you can spell out exactly who is invited and be sure you get confirmation on who will be there.

When you have a finalized guest list, think about the seating arrangements at the dinner. Place cards aren't necessary but may be helpful at particularly large rehearsal dinners. This is a good chance for both sets of parents to sit together and get acquainted. The same goes for the members of the bridal party.

## Gift-Giving and Receiving

The rehearsal dinner is not the place for the bride and groom to accept gifts. On the contrary, this is often the time that the wedding couple showers their families and attendants with gifts of thanks for being a part of their celebration. Gifts should be given to both sets of parents, as well as everyone in the wedding party.

Several toasts probably will be given, starting with the host of the dinner (typically the groom's father). Others are welcome to toast the couple, including the best man and maid of honor. Before the night is over, the bride and groom should say a few words of thanks.

# Post-Wedding Parties

By the time you tie the knot, chances are you may have been the guest of honor at an engagement party, a couple bridal showers, a bachelor party, and a rehearsal dinner. You finally get to the main event—the wedding reception—and think you're done. As crazy as it seems, that's often not the case.

If you've planned a late-morning or early afternoon wedding and reception, you'll probably have out-of-town guests and extended family members who want to continue the festivities after the reception is over. Parents of either the bride or groom (typically whoever lives in or near the town where the wedding takes place) might host a post-wedding party. This is not a necessary event but is a nice way to gather one last time and reminisce about the nuptials that just took place. You should make every effort to attend, but you need not stay long. If your honeymoon plans clash with post-wedding parties, everyone will understand.

If your reception is in the evening, your parents might want to host a post-wedding brunch or breakfast the morning after the wedding. This can be as simple as spreading the word to your wedding party that everyone is meeting for breakfast at the hotel restaurant at a given time. Typically the parents of the bride pick up the tab for such an event, so be sure to talk to them before you invite anyone who might not be on their list.

The post-wedding brunch need not include everyone who's staying at the hotel. After a super-hectic weekend, it's a good idea to keep the guest list to a minimum—immediate family only, perhaps, or just those in the wedding party.

If you're too exhausted to attend, be gracious and contact the host to give them your thanks and your regrets.

**6**

# The Rules of Receptions

## In This Chapter

- Creating a reception seating plan
- Picking the menu
- Cutting the cake
- Dancing do's and don'ts
- "Toast! Toast!" and other reception entertainment

It's easy for brides and grooms to use the "it's my wedding and I'll do what I want" excuse for any and all decisions along the way. But I'm here to tell you that there actually are a few tried-and-true right and wrong ways of doing things, and you'd be wise to err on the side of tradition in some circumstances.

In this chapter, I tell you about some common etiquette rules for wedding receptions, including the food, drinks, and special dances. I also help you figure out where everyone should sit and how to serve your guests.

# Musical Chairs

Part of planning a decent party is being sure everyone in attendance will be comfortable. So if you're serving food that's more substantial than buttered hors d'oeuvres, each guest must have a seat. Granted, chances are extremely slim that every single guest will be sitting down at the same time, but don't use that as an excuse to skimp on the number of chairs you rent or the size of the banquet hall you select. People use their seats as their own little "home base" throughout the reception—it's a place to put their jacket or purse, to stash their wedding favor and program, and to sit and enjoy their slice of cake. Don't deny them this tiny pleasure.

Even during a cocktail hour, when nearly all guests are comfortable standing and mingling, be sure at least a few tables and seats are available for your oldest guests, those who are pregnant, or those who have special needs.

## Creating a Seating Plan

The smallest and most informal wedding receptions don't need ordered seating arrangements of any kind. Just be sure adequate seating is available. For larger and more formal receptions, however, you do need to provide some order if you'd like to avoid the chaos of 300 people trying to choose their own seats.

There are two types of assigned seating: *assigned tables* and *assigned seats*. If you're serving a buffet or a semiformal sit-down meal, assigned tables are

the way to go. You should have a table set up near
the front door with a place card for every guest,
arranged alphabetically by last name. Include
on the place card the table number that guest is
assigned to. Arrange the table numbers in the
middle of each table. Be sure they're large enough
to be read fairly easily from both sides of the room.
And number the tables in a logical order so your
guests don't have to hunt for their assigned table.

### Wedded Bliss

It's helpful to place a simple diagram
of the room with the table numbers
clearly marked next to the place cards at
the entrance to the reception room.

When deciding who should sit where, keep the big
picture in mind and use common sense. It might
not be wise to sit your alcoholic uncle right next to
the bar. And your grandmother probably won't be
very comfortable right in front of the DJ's booth
and speakers. Seat families with small children
at tables with easy access to the restrooms. If the
dance floor cuts the room in half, seat guests of
both the bride and groom on each side to encour-
age mingling.

If you're having a very formal reception and would
like to have assigned seating, you must provide
a seating chart—one at each entrance to the
reception hall, if possible—that lists the guests
alphabetically with the table number where they're
assigned. Individual name cards should then be

placed above the dessert spoon and fork at each table setting, with the table number prominently displayed at the center of each table. Again, make it as easy as possible for your guests to find their seat.

### Wedded Bliss

On the place cards, use first and last names. Also, write the guest's name on *both* sides of the card so people sitting across from them can see who they're talking to.

Assigned seating is done in the best interest of your guests, so whenever possible, seat guests in a male-female-male pattern around each table. And use careful consideration when drawing up a diagram of the room and placing people together.

The first few tables often are easy to fill; grandparents, aunts, uncles, and cousins are natural choices for shared tables. But then it gets harder. Consider interests, personalities, and ages when assigning strangers to dine together. You can mix guests of the groom and guests of the bride. Seat single guests together, but try to avoid an exclusively single-guest table, as that might make your single friends feel like outcasts. Instead, seat a few single friends at a table with a few of their married friends, if possible.

If you have 12 college pals to seat at tables for 10, split them evenly between two tables, and at each of those tables assign 2 couples who know each other, preferably ones who are near in age to your college friends, too.

If you're inviting children and many are similar ages, you can seat them together at a kids' table. But keep their parents at tables close by.

## VIP Tables

At wedding receptions, your guests' attention will be directed to you throughout the night. They'll be raising their glasses to toast to your future and doing silly things to get you to kiss each other. Therefore, you should be seated at a head table that is centrally located and easily seen from all corners of the room.

### Bridal Blunder

At your reception, whether you're at a table on a raised platform or not, you are definitely on display. You are setting the example for acceptable behavior at your party, so behave.

Some brides and grooms wish to dine alone at a sweetheart's table. If you do this, your honor attendants and parents should be at VIP tables to your left and right. Seat the attendants' spouses with them as well.

If you prefer to share your head table with your honor attendants, the two of you should sit next to each other with the best man seated next to the bride and the maid of honor seated next to the groom. If you have more than those two attendants, seat the rest of the attendants around the table in groomsman-bridesmaid-groomsman fashion. Junior honor attendants typically sit with their parents, not at the head table. If you have both a maid and matron of honor, seat the maid of honor next to the groom and the matron of honor between two groomsmen at the same table.

This type of head table traditionally is raised from the floor and the entire bridal party sits facing the guests. Although some consider this setup a bit dated, it is in keeping with tradition and is a fine choice if that's what you'd like. The head table may be decorated with your bridal bouquet and the bridesmaids' bouquets, but be sure your guests can still see you clearly.

You may also choose to have a four-person head table just for you, your spouse, the best man, and the maid of honor. If so, the rest of the attendants should be seated at a table beside yours. Seating their spouses with them is optional and usually depends on how many seats you have per table.

Yet another option for a head table is to sit with your spouse and both sets of parents. This is rarely done but works well for small, intimate receptions.

If seating parents at a separate table, the parents of the bride and groom may be seated at the same table, along with the wedding officiant and his or her spouse. You could also seat both sets of parents at separate head tables with their respective family members. Both of these tables should be front and center, the closest to the bride and groom's head table. Unless they have an unusually healthy relationship, seat divorced parents at separate tables with their respective friends and family.

**History of Love**

Tradition states that because the bride's parents are hosting the party, they sit at opposite ends of the table. This isn't a hard-and-fast rule, though.

# Bon Appétit

What's a party without food? No matter what time of day your wedding reception takes place, no matter how tight your budget or how small your guest list, it's imperative that you serve your guests something to eat and drink.

## What to Serve

At the very least, you should serve wedding cake and coffee. At the very most, well, the sky's the limit.

Many afternoon and evening wedding receptions begin with a cocktail hour, at which time either plated or butlered hors d'oeuvres (either hot or cold) are served. This is a good idea if you and your bridal party will be delayed in getting to the reception because you're having post-wedding photographs taken.

> **Wedded Bliss**
>
> If you're having a cocktail hour for your guests to enjoy while your bridal party is being photographed, have some hors d'oeuvres and drinks set aside in a small room for your bridal party once you arrive.

The food is served after the bridal party is announced and any blessing is given. The bride and groom should be served first or lead the buffet line. Then the wedding party is served, followed by the parents of the bride and groom, and then the rest of the crowd.

Many cultures have ethnic dishes that are traditionally served for celebratory events such as weddings. Talk to the parents on both sides to see if they would like to serve anything special. It's up to them to provide enough of the dish or treat for everyone in attendance, so give them an accurate head count.

## Everybody Dance ... *Now?*

It's up to the bride and groom to signal when it's okay to dance. You may dance with your new spouse between courses or, if the mood strikes, right in the middle of the meal. Just be aware that whatever you do sets the example for your guests to follow.

## They're Cutting the Cake!

At full-meal receptions, the wedding cake is served just after lunch or dinner; at afternoon tea receptions, it's served immediately after the guests arrive and are greeted.

The groom places his hand over the bride's, and together they cut a piece from the bottom tier of the cake. They then feed each other a bite from this slice. This tradition symbolizes their willingness to share in their new life together, so think twice before you smash the cake in your new spouse's face. That's not only poor manners, it's also not a very good way to start your marriage—symbolically or otherwise. And believe me: you *do not* want to be the unlucky groom who smears raspberry creme filling all over his bride's wedding gown.

### Wedded Bliss

If you want to save some of your wedding cake, defrost it and eat it on your one-month anniversary. Or don't save it at all, but return to the baker on your one-year anniversary and order a small cake using the same flavors you had at your wedding. That's a much tastier tradition.

After the bride and groom taste the cake, the bride serves slices to her new in-laws and the groom does the same to his. Then the caterer takes the cake back to the kitchen to cut and serve to the rest of the guests. In less-formal affairs, you may designate a few people to cut and serve your cake.

# Entertain Me

You will, without a doubt, have fun at your wedding reception simply because it's your party. Everyone you love is there, people will compliment you all night long, and you get to leave the party with the love of your life. Making sure you have a good time is not really necessary; it's a given.

However, a few little traditions help move the party along and entertain the myriad guests you've invited who may not be told over and over how gorgeous they look and how lucky they are.

## Special Dances

Many brides dream about dancing with their spouse and then with their dad on their wedding day. It's one of those quintessential wedding moments. They imagine adoring loved ones looking on, "Isn't she lovely?" comments whispered, and cameras flashed to capture the sentimentality of it all.

Even if your spouse says he "doesn't dance," if you're having a formal reception, it's important that this tradition be upheld. People expect to see you dance. It needn't be a perfectly choreographed waltz; simply swaying in each other's arms to the sounds of your favorite love song will do.

The bride and groom's first dance as husband and wife often happens immediately after they're introduced and enter the reception hall, before any toast is given or eating commences. The first dance also may take place after the first course of a very formal meal, before the main course is served.

After the bride and groom dance, sometimes they invite the bridal party onto the dance floor for a second song. Bridesmaids and groomsmen don't have to dance with each other, though. If they all have spouses in attendance, they may invite their spouses to dance with them. Or you can skip this dance entirely. Do what will make your bridal party most comfortable.

Other special dances include the father of the bride dancing with his daughter and the groom dancing with his mother. There is no particular song you must dance to. Choose a favorite from your childhood or one that speaks to your heart. Sometime during the night the bride should also dance with the groom's father and the groom should dance with the bride's mother. These dances need not be announced.

If you're planning a Jewish wedding reception, you probably will be dancing the Horah. The Horah is an Israeli folk dance in which guests hold hands and dance around in a circle while the bride and groom are hoisted up on chairs in the center. This dance is done after dinner has been cleared, when the party is in full swing.

This is also the time for other ethnic dances and any sort of lively group or line dance initiated by the DJ.

**Bridal Blunder**

The "dollar dance," where men line up and pay a dollar (sometimes giving as much as $10 or $20) to dance with the bride for a few seconds, is in poor taste. It's basically asking your guests for money, which is not something a good party hostess does.

## Toasts and Speeches

Traditionally, the best man gives the first toast to the wedding couple after the receiving line and the introduction of the wedding party and before the meal commences. The best man should stand, but the bride and groom and the rest of the guests should be seated for this toast. Be sure every guest has been offered a glass of champagne or an alternate beverage before handing over the microphone to the best man.

Afterward, the groom should stand and thank his best man and then offer a toast to his bride and both sets of parents. Then the bride may offer a toast to her groom and the hosts of the reception (traditionally her parents).

Sometimes the maid of honor would also like to offer a toast to the new couple, although she is not required to do so. Other toasts or speeches that follow include ones by the parents of both bride and groom and other relatives or special friends.

Be welcoming to the toasters, but keep the time for toasts and speeches to a minimum. Your guests are no doubt hungry and anxious to get on with the party.

The hosts of the reception should be the last to speak. They should thank everyone for coming and give a nod to the bride and groom. They might also introduce the clergy member if he or she will give a blessing before the meal.

## Please Join Me in Prayer

It's common for a blessing to be given before the meal is served at a wedding reception. Often the clergyman who officiated your wedding does the honors. If you have a member of the family who is particularly spiritual, asking them to give a blessing is a nice way to include them in your festivities.

### Wedded Bliss

Be sure your bridal party are on their best behavior during the prayer—mouths closed and heads bowed.

Whoever you'd like to do this honor, be sure to ask them beforehand, and give them a 5-minute warning so they're not caught standing in line at the bar or in the restroom when the moment arrives! Also, ask that the blessing be respectful of the myriad beliefs your guests might have and to keep it brief.

At Jewish weddings, a special blessing called a hamotzi is given over a braided loaf of bread called challah, which is then passed around to the guests.

## Garters and Bouquets

Late in the reception the bride and groom may choose to do the traditional garter and bouquet toss. This is not a mandatory reception element, however. Some bashful brides don't want their new husbands crawling up their skirts to retrieve a stitch of lace—while every eye in the room watches. And there might not be enough single gals or guys in the crowd to catch a bouquet tossed behind the bride's back. Also, sometimes cultural considerations prevent even a bride and groom from such intimate displays of affection in public.

If you do want to toss the bouquet but hate to see it given away, ask your florist to make a small "breakaway bouquet" that separates from the main bouquet. Or the florist can create a separate arrangement that mimics your bouquet but on a much smaller scale.

Even though you might think this is a fun tradition, your single friends might not want the spotlight shined on them. Do not pull, yank, or otherwise coax your single friends to be a part of the bouquet or garter toss. Their participation is up to them, not you.

Chapter **7**

# Small Details, Big Effects

## In This Chapter

- Receiving line rules
- Making guests feel special
- Thanking loved ones
- Tipping vendors

By now you've got all the big decisions made and your wedding day seems to be coming together nicely. After you've done so much work it's easy to sit back and say, "I'm done!" But any good party host knows that it's those last little touches that guests remember and perhaps appreciate most at the end of the day.

In this chapter, I tell you what you can do to treat your guests like they're special. I show you who should greet guests in the receiving line, what types of favors and other things will make your guests feel most welcome, and how best to thank the loved ones who are making all this possible. I also tell you who you should be tipping at the end of the day, and—provided they've done a great job—how much they should get.

# The Receiving Line

Immediately after the wedding, your guests will be bursting to congratulate you, and you'll be eager to greet all the loved ones who just witnessed your nuptials. The receiving line is a traditional way for you to greet each guest—something you may not have time to do later if your reception is very large.

## The Where of Receiving Lines

The proper place for a receiving line is at the entrance to the reception. This is traditionally where brides and grooms and their parents usually greeted their guests as they arrived, just as you would greet someone at your front door as they arrive for your party.

However, nowadays many couples spend considerable time at the ceremony site taking formal photographs, so their guests beat them to the reception site. If you think you'll get caught up at the ceremony site and not make it to the reception site on time, form the receiving line right after your ceremony.

## Who's Who in Receiving Lines

Whoever is hosting the wedding should stand first in line. Often this is the bride's mother. The bride's father may stand beside her, but his participation is optional. Some families opt to send the father on to the reception to ensure everything is ready and to greet guests as they arrive.

Next in line is the mother of the groom, followed by the father of the groom, whose participation, again, is optional. If the bride's father won't be in the receiving line, the groom's father should opt out as well. The groom's parents stand next to the bride and groom.

If your reception is very large and you have many guests to greet, keep the receiving line to these six (or four) people. If your wedding is more intimate, you may include the maid of honor, who stands next to the groom.

So the line, in order, should be as follows:

1. Mother of the bride
2. Father of the bride (optional)
3. Mother of the groom
4. Father of the groom (optional)
5. Bride
6. Groom
7. Maid of honor (optional)

You may also include the rest of the bridesmaids and the groomsmen, if you wish. Keep in mind that the more people there are to greet, the longer the whole tradition will take and the later you all will get to your reception. If you are including the rest of your wedding party, they stand after the maid of honor in a male-female-male pattern.

Children who are in the wedding party should not be part of the receiving line. If the kids are the bride's or groom's own children, they may be given a separate duty that makes them feel important, like standing with the guest book at a nearby table, or sitting with the bride's flowers while she greets her guests.

> **Wedded Bliss**
>
> Set up your guest book at a small table at the end of the receiving line or near the reception hall entrance so all your guests see and sign it. Position it far enough away from the line so it doesn't create a bottleneck of people, though.

## In Cases of Divorced Parents

Divorced parents shouldn't stand in the line together. It doesn't matter if they're okay with it; it would just confuse some of the guests as they're making their way through the line. The parent and stepparent who have spent the most time with the bride (or groom), or the ones giving the wedding, should stand in the line. If you're worried that the other set of parents might feel slighted, ask them to prepare a toast to the couple at the beginning of the reception.

If divorced parents are not remarried, the mother should stand in the line and the father may greet guests separately at the reception. If both of the bride's parents are remarried and both are hosting the wedding, they should both be included in the receiving line, separated by the groom's parents.

However, if the bride's parents are divorced and her father is hosting the wedding, then by all means he should be in the receiving line. He should stand next to the groom at the end of the line, along with his wife if he's remarried.

## Receiving Line Etiquette

The receiving line is not the place to give wedding guests a complete history of how you found your wedding gown. A quick handshake or hug and a warm but very brief greeting are all that's called for here. The bride should thank her guests for coming, tell them how happy she is to see them, and introduce them to her groom if they haven't yet met.

It works best if each person in the receiving line turns and introduces the guest to the next person in the line, so the guest doesn't have to introduce himself several times in a row. ("John, this is my Aunt Betty, my mother's sister.")

One final note about receiving lines: even if you form a receiving line to greet your guests, you're still expected to make every effort to walk from table to table to greet your guests during the reception. The receiving line is good insurance in case any guests aren't seated when you make it to their table.

# A Touch of Class

I have a friend who throws the best parties. In addition to the usual party dips and excellent music mixes, she pays attention to little details that leave a lasting impression. Small bowls of chocolate liqueurs can be found on her coffee table. There are always fresh flowers in the bathroom. And nobody ever leaves without a parting gift, whether it's a New Year's noisemaker or a frosted cupcake for the road.

Little touches like these make guests feel not just welcome, but special. This is how you want your guests to feel as they leave your wedding reception. These items don't have to cost an arm and a leg, but believe me, you'll get a lot of mileage out of whatever you do spend.

## Restroom Baskets

Ever get to a wedding reception, break a nail, and then spend the next five hours trying not to snag your pantyhose? Ever indulge in the garlic-encrusted shrimp hors d'oeuvres only to wish you had some mouthwash before the dancing portion of the party began?

Wedding receptions, whether for 50 or 500, should feel like intimate family affairs, not anonymous assembly line events. You want your guests to feel as comfortable as they would if they were at your own home. A simple way to do this is to provide restroom baskets with toiletries and other useful items for your guests to use.

Check with the reception hall manager first to be sure it's okay to leave something in each restroom and then head to your local drug store for some travel-size items. These items will no doubt save the day for at least a few wedding guests with bad luck—or bad breath.

### Wedded Bliss

Buy thick decorative or white dispos-able towels to place by the sink if the reception site's restroom only offers an electric hand-dryer or industrial brown paper towel rolls. You can also bring a bottle of nice hand soap (and matching scented lotion, for the women's restroom) if the reception site has nothing but the typical industrial pink variety.

Use a large basket and tie a ribbon in your wedding color scheme to the handle. Fill it with items your guests would find useful, such as these for women:

- Antacids
- Bobby pins
- Breath mints or gum
- Clear nail polish
- Comb/brush
- Deodorant
- Hairspray
- Hand lotion
- Mouthwash (pro-vide small cups, too)
- Nail file
- Safety pins
- Small Band-Aids
- Stain remover wipes/pen
- Tampons/ panty liners
- Tissues

Items appropriate for a guest basket for men include the following:

- Antacids
- Breath mints or gum
- Comb
- Deodorant
- Disposable razor
- Mouthwash (provide small cups, too)
- Small Band-Aids
- Tissues

Give these baskets to a couple close friends who are not in the wedding party and, therefore, will be headed directly to the reception after the wedding. It's best to choose a male and female to help you with this, so they can both enter their appropriate restrooms without getting any funny looks (or surprised guests!).

## Out-of-Towner Gift Bags

Friends and family who come from out of town to attend your wedding do so with considerable sacrifice of time, energy, and money. They most likely had to miss at least one day of work, pay for travel expenses and accommodations, and find their way around an unfamiliar town. The least you can do is make them feel welcome as soon as they arrive in town. The best way to do this is to leave small gift bags at the front desk of the hotels where your guests are staying.

If you've blocked a number of rooms at various hotels near your reception site, you can find out how many of those rooms have been booked by your wedding guests. Once this number matches your RSVP guest list, you know how many gift bags you need to make and where they should be delivered.

### Wedded Bliss

Include a little something extra (a travel-size bottle of their favorite liquor, for example) for those in the wedding party, along with an itinerary of their wedding party duties (rehearsal time, rehearsal dinner place and time, etc.).

The bags need not be elaborate, nor their contents expensive. Here are a few ideas of what to include:

- A couple bottles of water
- Snacks (Buy snack bags of chips, pretzels, or peanuts in bulk at your local grocery store.)
- A map of the area
- Brochures of touristy things to see and do in town
- A copy of the directions to the ceremony and reception sites that you included in the invitation
- Any small goodie your town or state is known for

Tie the bag's handles together with a festive ribbon and affix a simple note that reads "Welcome to our wedding weekend. So glad you could join us!" signed by you and your soon-to-be spouse. If you only have a few out-of-towners, you can personalize them by addressing each bag with the person's name.

## Fun with Wedding Favors

Many people believe that wedding favors for your guests are a mandatory part of the evening. They are not. They are, however, a nice way for people to leave with a small token of your appreciation for their presence—not to mention a tangible memory of your big day.

Favors need not be elaborate, but they are at many weddings. They also can show a little of your personality and add a touch of whimsy to the party. I know of a couple who rented a photo booth and allowed guests to take strips of keepsake photos of themselves, free of charge. The line for the photo booth was longer than the line for the bar!

Before you decide on what favor you'd like to give, do some research and shop around for the best prices. Remember that some guests will forget to even take the favor with them when they leave, so don't buy anything so expensive or make anything so time-consuming that you'll be hurt if a dozen are left on the tables when the lights come up at the end of the night.

### History of Love

The most common traditional wedding favor is five jordan almonds wrapped in tulle.

You can find numerous favor ideas out there, especially online and in bridal planning magazines. Here are a few standard ones:

- Fragrant soaps or bath salts
- Hershey's Hugs and Kisses, wrapped in tulle
- Flower bulbs
- Small picture frames
- Miniature bottles of wine or champagne, printed with the bride and groom's own label
- Take-home boxes with small slices of wedding cake or a cupcake
- Decorated flowerpots
- CDs with the wedding song and special labels
- Flowers
- Lottery tickets
- Small bottles of bubbles to blow at the bride and groom as they leave the reception

Wedding favors should be simple, but they should have some significant meaning, whether it be a reflection of the newly married couple's life together; the wedding theme; or something that symbolizes the state, town, or season in which the wedding took place.

## "We Have So Many People to Thank ..."

People like to be recognized, even if it is *your* day. A good party host makes a mental note about anybody in attendance who is celebrating something special. For instance, if you're getting married during peak wedding season, chances are a few of your wedding guests are celebrating their anniversary within days of your wedding day. Remember to acknowledge them with a brief pause in the festivities as you toast to their marriage. If you can, find out what their wedding song is and request that it be played for them.

Likewise, note any birthdays or other special occasions your loved ones might be celebrating. They probably won't be heralding the news too publicly for fear of stealing your spotlight, but they no doubt would appreciate the fact that, amid all your excitement, you cared enough to remember them.

It's also good manners to publicly acknowledge those friends and professionals who have made your wedding what it is. A shout-out to the reception hall staff after a delicious dinner with excellent service is much appreciated. Toward the beginning of the reception, take a moment to thank anyone who assisted with the music or decorations at the ceremony.

Finally, small tokens of your appreciation should be given to loved ones who offered their professional services for free or at a discounted rate. Musicians, photographers, florists, soloists—anyone who you know personally should be thanked with a small gift. This can be as simple as a basket of scented candles and bath salts or a gift certificate to a local restaurant.

# Tipping Vendors

Tipping is something that needlessly stresses people out. Often it seems like the only person who knows who should be tipped, and how much, is the professional providing the service.

**Wedded Bliss**

Gifts are not appropriate for hired professionals with whom you have a signed contract. Those folks are tipped for a job well done.

Your wedding budget should include cash for tipping vendors and other professionals. If your parents (or someone else) are paying for the wedding, be sure they're aware of this wedding day expense.

But before you start doling out dollars, check all the contracts that you've signed and invoices you've received. Gratuities are included on the bill at most hotels, country clubs, and restaurants. Be careful not to double-tip wait staff, bartenders, or the maître d'. And if a tip is included in your bill, ask the manager which employees this covers and which it does not. Your caterer, for example, may need to be tipped separately.

The following are guidelines for what to tip. Keep in mind that tipping is higher in metropolitan areas. When in doubt, ask your wedding planner how much someone usually gets.

- *Porters:* at least $2 per bag
- *Restroom attendants:* $1 per guest
- *Parking attendants:* $1 per car
- *Limousine driver:* 15 to 20 percent of the bill (Check to be sure gratuity isn't already included on the bill.)
- *Bartenders:* 10 to 15 percent of the liquor bill, or $50 per bartender
- *Waiters/waitresses:* $10 to $20 per person
- *Delivery driver for florist, baker, etc.:* $5 to $10 each
- *Caterer/hotel banquet manager/club manager:* 15 to 20 percent of the food and drink bill
- *Hair stylists/makeup artists/nail technicians:* 15 to 20 percent

**Bridal Blunder**

Wedding guests often think they need to bring tip money for the bar, even if it's an open bar. But chances are the bartender's gratuity (typically 10 to 15 percent of the liquor bill) is built into the reception hall bill that you'll receive at the end of the night. If that's the case, don't allow the bartender to set up a tip jar during your reception.

Clergy, wedding planners, and photographers/ videographers *do not* receive tips. You may make a donation to the church or synagogue if you want.

Although technically all tipping is optional, some tipping is expected. The following professionals are not expecting a tip but would certainly appreciate one if you find their services to be exceptional:

- *Musicians/DJ:* $20 to $25 each
- *Soloists/organist:* Whatever you feel is appropriate
- *Paid officiant:* 15 to 20 percent

# Chapter 8

# Presents, Please

## In This Chapter

- Using gift registries
- Bridal shower etiquette
- Choosing gifts for the bridal party
- Writing thank you notes

Let's face it: one of the immediate perks of getting married is getting lots of gifts. Boxes begin arriving at your door weeks before the wedding, and thick envelopes continue to trickle in to your mailbox for weeks afterward. This, of course, is loads of fun, but there's a right way and a wrong way to go about asking for, accepting, and acknowledging wedding gifts.

In this chapter, I give you information on what to register for and how you should—and shouldn't—tell people about your bridal registry. I also help you figure out what gifts to give to the people who are standing up for you on your wedding day, and I review the ancient art of the thank you note and just what kinds of rewards the ritual reaps.

# The Joy of Gift Registries

Gift registries are magical things. They're like wish lists for your dream home. The mere thought of them can conjure up daydreams of dinner parties and holiday family get-togethers. There's an art to creating and managing a bridal gift registry that, when done properly, virtually assures you of opening lots of gifts you'd hoped for without offending a single gift-giver.

And here's a time to get your guy involved! Many grooms have only a passing interest in the endless details of wedding planning—until the day you start talking about gift registries. Then, suddenly, they're the world's most eager helper! Guys are usually thrilled to accompany their brides on this—and *only* this—wedding planning excursion. They beg to be the one to hold the scanner gun so they can zap, zap, zap all sorts of home-improvement tools and expensive electronics onto the registry. It's great to get the groom involved, but it's essential that a bride keep her registry—and her beau—realistic.

## Where to Register

It seems every store you enter these days has the capability of setting up a gift registry. Gone are the days when large department stores were the only option. Now people register at stores ranging from Wal-Mart and The Home Depot to specialty boutiques and Internet-only shops. Where is the right place for you to register?

### Bridal Blunder

Printing "No gifts, please" on the invitations is a no-no. It's seen as presumptuous, because you're implying that your guests were expected to bring gifts until you told them otherwise. Do not include any mention of gifts—whether or not to give, what to give, or where to send them—on your invitations. Rely on word of mouth instead.

First, consider your personalities and the types of things you need—or are just dreaming about! If you and your fiancé are just setting up a home, an all-inclusive department store like JCPenney or a discount department store like Target is a good idea. There you can select everything from towels to toasters.

On the other hand, if you've been living together for a few years, you already have the basics and might want to concentrate on registering for fine china, crystal, and silver. These are extravagant extras that probably weren't a priority when you moved in together but will come in handy when you host family get-togethers and holiday celebrations in the coming years.

Whatever you decide, select one or two places the majority of your guests have access to. Although many people do their gift shopping online, some prefer to go to the store to purchase your gift and have it wrapped. Try to pick at least one store that's located in most major cities—or at least in your hometown, where your Great Aunt Edna will be shopping.

Fine china is a traditional gift registry item, but keep your lifestyle in mind when selecting such pieces. Don't be afraid to register for more contemporary or casual dinnerware if you think you'll get more use out of them than fine bone china. You want to use and enjoy the gifts you get—not merely store them in a cabinet.

### Wedded Bliss

Try to keep china, crystal, and silverware on a single store's registry to make it easier to track how many settings you've received and eliminate confusion about returns if you receive too many.

Also, keep in mind that your wedding guests have wide-ranging budgets and tastes, so select items in several different price points. Don't assume friends and loved ones will pool their money for ultra-expensive gifts you select.

Although registries were created primarily for wedding gifts, many people use them for bridal shower gifts as well. Be sure to have plenty to choose from in the $30 price range.

As it gets closer to your wedding date, it's a good idea to check your registry and add items if the pickings are getting slim or several choices are now unavailable or out of stock. Many people do their shopping in the two weeks prior to the wedding. You want them to have plenty of gifts to choose from so they're not forced to find something else in the store they hope you might like.

## When to Register

It's okay to register for gifts as soon as you announce your engagement. But keep in mind that if your engagement period is longer than six months, some of the items you register for might not be available when your wedding rolls around. Remember that with the changing seasons, store selections change, too.

If you're not in a big hurry to register, don't fret. I'm sure you have more important wedding-related details to hammer out before deciding on a china pattern. But do try to have a gift registry set up by the time you mail your save-the-date cards. And you certainly must have your registry finalized by the time your wedding invitations go out.

### Wedded Bliss

Many stores that sell china and crystal keep your gift registry open for up to 2 years. This makes it easy for family to check to see how many settings you still need when shopping for birthday and Christmas gifts later.

## Spreading the Word

Creating your registry is the easy part; telling people about it can be a bit trickier. Wedding guests like to have the option of using a gift registry because it takes the guesswork out of shopping for the perfect gift. But they don't like being told what to give the bride and groom or where they have to shop.

The biggest rule to keep in mind here is that it's not appropriate to give people your registry information on either save-the-date cards or wedding invitations. Save that for bridal shower invitations.

# Gifts for Your Bridal Party

When you ask someone to be in your wedding, you're asking them to make quite a commitment—both of time and money. This is true for all but the most modest nuptials.

Your bridal party folks are the ones who will make sure you're ready and looking your best for your big day. They're the ones who will hold the rings, carry your flowers, bustle your dress, give you planning advice when you ask, and toast to your new life together. Clearly, these people need to be properly thanked.

## Attendants' Gifts

It's up to the bride to give a small token of her appreciation to each of her attendants. Likewise, the groom is responsible for thanking his groomsmen with a small gift. These gifts need not be extravagant or expensive, but they should have some special meaning or be personalized for each attendant.

Traditionally, each bridesmaid or usher receives the same gift (although they may be monogrammed to give each a personal touch). It's acceptable, however, for each attendant to be given a different gift, something that you select based on their individual tastes and personality. The best man and maid of honor are sometimes given a little something extra for their extra-special role in the wedding.

It's okay to give your bridesmaids a necklace or other such accessory that you'd like them to wear for your wedding. But unless the accessory is something they will definitely wear again some other time, you should also get them something separate that they can enjoy long after they shed their bridesmaid dresses. A few other appropriate gifts are picture frames, engraved photo boxes, and monogrammed tote bags or purses.

### Bridal Blunder

Don't think of your attendants as one group but as individuals. It's easy to get swept up in the business of choosing something unique and personalizing it for each person, only to forget that you're buying earrings for a woman who doesn't have pierced ears or a sterling silver flask for a man who doesn't drink.

Typical groomsmen gifts include engraved money clips, flasks, pewter mugs, and key chains. A bottle of fine scotch or wine and gift certificates to rounds of golf are also appropriate, but know your groomsmen's taste and hobbies before getting something so distinct.

Don't forget the others in your wedding party; everyone—including ring bearers, flower girls, and junior bridesmaids—should be given a gift. Children in the wedding party might enjoy receiving a charm bracelet; computer game; or gift certificate to a movie theater, pizza parlor, or children's amusement venue.

## Parents' Gifts

Your wedding day is a bittersweet one for your parents. No matter how long you've been out of the house and living on your own, there's something about seeing your child get married that marks the end of your role as central figure in your child's life. In some strange way, your childhood is over as soon as you say "I do." Parents know this, and although they rejoice with your good fortune, they silently mourn the shift in their role in your life.

To ease this transition and to thank them—whether that thank you is for raising you in a healthy environment or footing the bill for your entire wedding—it's a nice idea to give your parents a gift before your wedding. You may give them one gift they can enjoy as a couple or individual gifts for both mom and dad.

Your mom might enjoy a bottle of perfume, spa gift certificate, or fresh flowers delivered to her door the morning of your wedding. For dad, gift certificates for golf, a bottle of fine scotch, cuff links, or monogrammed handkerchiefs are typically well received. Appropriate couple gifts include a retouched, framed photo from their wedding day, a case of their favorite wine, or an engraved frame for your wedding photo.

The gifts for your parents need not be expensive, but they should be accompanied by a handwritten note from you expressing your gratitude for all they've done for you. If they're like most parents, they'll treasure that note even more than the gift you give them.

If your parents are remarried, be sure to keep your stepmother or stepfather in mind when buying a gift, depending on how close you are to them and how involved they've been in planning your wedding.

## Gifts for Others

It's not mandatory for you to give gifts to absolutely everyone who participates in your wedding. The soloist, junior usher, and guest book attendant need only a kind word of thanks and perhaps a corsage or boutonniere.

However, gift-giving (and paying for said gifts) is up to you. If you're feeling generous, you may present them with a small token of your gratitude.

Keep in mind that whatever you give them should be a good deal less extravagant than what you give your bridesmaids and groomsmen.

# Thank You!

Thank you notes might seem like an afterthought, but they are extremely important. What you write in the note is not nearly as important as your actual sending of the thank you note. And the quicker, the better.

Sending a thank you note to a gift-giver acknowledges that you received their gift and that you appreciate their generosity. It doesn't matter whether you opened a wedding gift in front of the giver and thanked them in person. A written note should be sent for every gift received.

You'll often hear lazy brides and grooms say that they have up to a year after the wedding to send thank you notes. That's not exactly true. The rule is that people have up to a year after the nuptials to *send* a wedding gift. Thank you notes should be sent within two weeks to one month from the time you receive the gift. The notes should be handwritten, not typed. And don't use cards with a preprinted message beyond "thank you."

These notes need not be too wordy or too detailed. It's far better to send a short note promptly than to let the notes stack up because you're unsure of how to compose the perfect letter. Remember, what you say isn't as important as the mere act of saying it.

### Bridal Blunder

E-mail is *not* the right venue to properly thank your loved ones for gifts. You may acknowledge receipt of a gift via e-mail the day you get it, but you must still send a formal, handwritten thank you note through the mail.

There are three points to writing a decent thank you note. First, acknowledge the gift. Then, tell the giver what will be done with the gift or how it will be used. Finally, tell the giver what their presence in your life and, presumably, at your wedding meant to you.

### Wedded Bliss

Write and send your shower thank you notes before the wedding. After the wedding, spend 10 minutes a day writing a note or two and mail them as you go. This keeps you from getting buried in unwritten correspondences. Be sure to keep a list of gifts you've received and notes you've sent. This list eventually will turn into a casual keepsake of all the presents you were blessed with.

Traditionally, the bride wrote out all the thank you notes. This is no longer a steadfast rule as more grooms pitch in and help. You can split the chore down the middle or otherwise share it in some way that makes sense to you. Do not, however, let them sit there because you're both stubbornly insisting that the other one write them!

Notes should be signed by the person writing it, although your spouse should be mentioned in the body of the letter. It's okay to use your first name only when writing to family and close friends. Use your first and last name (and possibly your maiden name as well) when signing thank you notes to people you don't know well.

# Returns and Exchanges

When you're getting a million gifts, chances are you'll receive a few duplicates or duds. Under certain circumstances it's okay to exchange gifts you don't care for or you already have. Use great tact when doing this, because you don't want anyone to think you didn't appreciate their thoughtfulness or they have bad taste.

If you've gotten duplicate gifts off your registry, by all means return the extras and use the money or credit to buy something you didn't get. But write the thank you notes to each sender for the original gift. If a guest buys you something that isn't from a registry, you might be stuck with it. If it's from someone who you're sure won't be visiting your house anytime in the foreseeable future, and you can find out where they got it, it's okay to return it. Be sure to send them a thank you note for the gift, although don't go into detail about how much you love it and where exactly you'll use it. You never want to get caught in a lie. A simple "thank you for such thoughtfulness" will do.

If you've been given something off the registry by someone who's fairly close to you, someone who will be coming to visit, you should hang onto the present. You needn't display it until the giver comes to visit.

# Broken Engagements

If things don't work out and the wedding is called off, any gifts you've received—even those that have been monogrammed—must be returned with a short note. You don't have to go into great detail, but some brief explanation for the return and a "thank you for sending it" is in order.

# When in Rome ...

## In This Chapter

- Respecting cultural differences
- Celebrating same-sex commitments
- Planning a military wedding

Weddings are as unique as the people who marry. You'll find plenty of variations on "traditional" weddings, and nearly all of those variations have their own etiquette guidelines.

In this chapter, I discuss a few different wedding scenarios where special etiquette rules apply. I go over how to blend two different cultures in one ceremony, how to word invitations to a ceremony for a same-sex couple, and how to choose who wears what in a military wedding.

## Cross-Cultural Affairs

In this day and age, couples of diverse backgrounds and beliefs are meeting and falling in love. It's not unusual to attend a wedding where officiants from two different faiths preside, or to be at a reception where food is served from cultures and countries on separate continents.

When planning your wedding, it's more than acceptable to blend your beliefs and culture with those of your mate—it's *essential*. It's also important that you follow the rules of good taste and check with your wedding officiant about any religious rules or stipulations.

## When to Bend Etiquette Rules

Addressing invitations to those outside the country can present a few cross-cultural challenges that go way beyond spelling foreign names correctly. For example, in the United States, if a wife is a doctor and her husband is not, she is listed first on the wedding invitation envelope. In many countries, however, it's insulting to list the woman before the man. Should you bend an etiquette rule to be sure you don't insult a wedding guest?

While bending a rule to spare someone's feelings is normally a good idea, this one brings with it a slippery slope of compromise. You could spend all day researching the cultures of all your wedding guests, and you'd have to go by different rules for all of them. The simplest way to avoid such a mess is to adhere to the etiquette rules in the country where the wedding is taking place.

## Embrace New Traditions

Maria and Eduardo chose to get married in Eduardo's native country, Mexico, because it was more financially feasible for Maria's family to travel there than for Eduardo's family to travel to the United States. But Maria wasn't prepared for the cultural differences in wedding etiquette. For one thing, she found that her Mexican invitees did not really believe RSVPing was necessary. She also discovered that they often showed up for weddings with other, uninvited guests in tow.

Just as she'd suspected, several people showed up to the wedding who hadn't RSVP'd, and others brought extended family members she hadn't invited.

But many guests also brought dishes of delicious homemade food and drinks to share, which is another party custom in Mexico. There was more than enough to feed everyone, and the authentic Mexican delicacies added to the charm and the family-friendly atmosphere Maria and Eduardo had hoped for.

### Wedded Bliss

The wedding favor is a good way to include a bit of your native culture in your wedding and give your guests a glimpse into your family's heritage.

Maria's problem was that she was trying to plan an American wedding in another country, applying all her familiar etiquette rules. When she truly embraced her Mexican marriage, however, she realized that her guests were not only exhibiting acceptable behavior, but they were also more gracious and generous than she could have hoped.

## Beware of Backfires

Sometimes well-meaning brides and grooms try to incorporate their mate's culture or family history into their otherwise traditional American wedding. This can reap rewards of goodwill from your mate's family, or it can backfire and insult the very people you are trying to include.

When Kelly was marrying Gary, she wanted to find a way to recognize Gary's German heritage in the ceremony. She planned to have the flower girls wear traditional Bavarian dresses, thinking this would bring a smile to her new in-laws' faces. But when she relayed her plans to Gary's sister, she was told that this would actually be seen as belittling and mocking German culture, as these costumes oversimplify Germany's rich culture.

Kelly was horrified, and thankful she'd asked someone "in the know" before going ahead with her idea. Scrapping the dress idea, she chose instead to include the Nurenberg Bridal Cup in their ceremony, which is an accepted German wedding tradition.

If you have an idea for how to incorporate another's religion or culture into your wedding, be sure to first ask a religious officiant or someone who's deeply familiar with that culture, language, or religious belief. Let them be your guide as to what's appropriate and tasteful.

## What's Faith Got to Do with It?

If the bride and groom are of different faiths, you can opt to marry in a nonreligious setting both of you find spiritual, such as outdoors under a stand of trees or by the ocean. Check with your officiant first, however, because not all clergy will conduct a wedding ceremony outside the church.

If you can't find a clergy member to preside over your outdoor wedding, it's perfectly acceptable to have a civil service and then have the marriage blessed by your clergy of choice. Again, check with your clergy member ahead of time to find out what is appropriate within your particular faith.

### Wedded Bliss

The keys to planning a proper interfaith ceremony are sensitivity, respect, and inclusiveness. You don't want anyone to feel alienated.

Here are some other acceptable options for interfaith couples trying to find a compromise for their nuptials:

- Have clergy from both faiths participate in the ceremony.
- Have a Unitarian Universalist clergy member perform the wedding.
- Have a friend marry you, which is possible now in several states. Call your county clerk to find out whether this is an option for you.

- Get married at city hall first and then conduct your own ceremony for extended family and friends using whatever religious passages and traditions are important to both of you.
- Have an interfaith minister perform the ceremony.

It's important to explain certain religious or cultural elements that many of your guests might not understand. You can do this in one of two ways: either the officiant can give a brief explanation for an element or expound on a religious passage's meaning when it's used in the ceremony, or you can briefly explain these elements in the program. Include some background information on anything you think your guests might want to know more about.

## Same-Sex Unions

Many gay partners are now holding civil ceremonies to celebrate their commitment to each other. Anytime two people want to pledge their lives together is a time to celebrate.

Often called *commitment ceremonies* or *affirmation ceremonies*, civil ceremonies for same-sex couples can have all the dignity and formality of wedding ceremonies for heterosexual couples. As with any party, etiquette is necessary to be sure all guests feel welcome and comfortable.

## Ceremony Essentials

Both sides may have honor attendants, although some brides and grooms wish to have both men and women stand up for both of them. If your honor attendants are mixed (some groomsmen are women, some bridesmaids are men), then select a bridesmaid gown and complementary groomsmen suit and let each attendant wear what he or she feels is appropriate.

When it comes to outfitting you and your partner, you should both wear what you find most comfortable, whether that means two women in bridal gowns or one opting for a dress and the other a feminine suit. Discuss your vision for your wedding with your partner and be sure you both will feel true to yourselves on your big day.

There may be two bachelor or bachelorette parties, giving each soon-to-be spouse his or her own special night out with friends.

## Guest Lists and Invitations

Making a guest list can be tricky for a same-sex couple, because not all your family and friends may be accepting and comfortable with such a public display of your love and lifestyle. Invite whomever you hope will come, knowing that some may decline the invitation. Better to invite them and be happily surprised at their support than not invite them because you think they'll disapprove, only to find out they were hurt by the snub.

Addressing invitations to a same-sex wedding should be done the same way any other wedding invitation is announced:

> The pleasure of your company
> is requested
> at the commitment ceremony for
> Mr. Paul Michael Adams
> and
> Mr. Jeffrey Thomas Brownstein
> Friday, the sixth of July
> at five o'clock
> Old Bay Art Gallery
> Nantucket, Massachusetts

Also, because same-sex commitment ceremonies are usually a bit less formal than traditional weddings, the style of your invitation should clue in your guests about how formal the event will be and what they should wear.

## Military Weddings

Military weddings are beautiful, formal affairs that have plenty of pomp and circumstance. Imagine walking under a canopy of raised swords while holding your new spouse's hand. How dramatic!

Kyle met Erin while both were in the Marine Corps stationed at Camp Pendleton, California. They wanted to take their time and plan the perfect wedding, but when Kyle was notified he was to be deployed to Iraq, they hit the fast forward button and moved up the ceremony by several months. The couple got married at the county courthouse with just their best friends in tow.

They planned to have a traditional ceremony and reception, with bridal showers and gifts and Erin walking up a real aisle, when Kyle returned. But when they researched such an option, they were surprised to learn that this setup—essentially having two weddings—breaks all the etiquette rules.

### Wedded Bliss

Different branches of the military have different rules for military weddings, so contact the protocol officer for your branch and find out what hoops, if any, you need to jump through to have the military wedding of your dreams.

Tons of military couples like Kyle and Erin assume they can have their cake now and, later, eat it, too. But etiquette states that once you're married, you're married. You cannot invite people to a second wedding just because you didn't get to wear a white gown when you actually got married.

You can invite people to a vow renewal (although this is usually reserved for people celebrating a special anniversary) or blessing of the marriage. This can be a beautiful, meaningful ceremony, but it's not a wedding. (For vow renewal etiquette, see Chapter 11.) You also can have a small wedding ceremony now and host a wedding reception with all the trimmings later.

## Ceremony and Reception Do's and Don'ts

It's a good idea to display the American flag some-where at your ceremony and/or reception site, as well as the standards of the military branch in which the bride and/or groom are serving. This is in addition to flowers.

> **Wedded Bliss**
>
> If you're getting married on a military base or at a military academy, go over your plans with the proper military authorities or military chaplain there. Get permission beforehand for decorations, flowers, and music.

The processional is the same as with a regular wed-ding, but the recessional may include the arch of swords or sabers. This arch is formed by an honor guard of commissioned officers in the military branch in which the groom or bride serves. The arch may be formed outside the wedding chapel or synagogue, depending on your preference and com-mon practices within that branch of the military.

At a seated military reception, military guests should be shown to their tables in order of rank.

## Dress Blues ... and Whites

A bride who is on active-duty military often faces a dilemma: should she wear the dress uniform she so proudly serves in, or should she wear the traditional white wedding gown she always dreamed of? Either is acceptable, so it's totally up to her. If she opts for the dress uniform, she still may carry a bouquet but she should not wear a veil.

When a bride wishes to wear a traditional gown and her groom and groomsmen will be in full dress uniforms, she should match her gown to that level of formality. An ankle-length dress and long train and veil will help her complement the formality of the men in her wedding party.

Military decorations replace boutonnieres on men's uniforms. Be sure your honor attendants know how formal the wedding is so they can wear the appropriate dress uniform, if they're also in the military. However, when only one or two members of your wedding party are military, it's best if they *not* wear their dress uniforms. If they do, they run the risk of catching everyone's attention, when all eyes should be focused on you! Your wedding party should look uniform, not be in different uniforms.

That said, if you want any of your honor attendants to be part of the honor guard that will create the arch of sabers, they need to be in full dress uniform. Only someone wearing the full dress uniform can carry a sword or saber.

## Military Wedding Invitations

Invitations are the first sign to guests that they have been invited to a military wedding. You can clue in your guests to this fact by including gold-braided edges or an image of crossed swords on the invitation.

The wording on the invitation should include the groom and/or bride's rank and service. The guest's, groom's, or bride's military title appears before his or her name only if he or she holds a rank equivalent to or higher than captain in the Army or commander in the Navy.

Mr. and Mrs. Patrick Evans Smith
request the honour of your presence
at the marriage of their daughter
Commander Jane Ann Smith
United States Navy
to
Major John David Jones
United States Marine Corps …

**Wedded Bliss**

Double-check all titles, rank, and branches or service before your calligrapher begins addressing your invitations.

If the bride or groom has a lesser rank, it is listed on the same line as the branch of service.

Mr. and Mrs. Patrick Evans Smith
request the honour of your presence
at the marriage of their daughter
Commander Jane Ann Smith
United States Navy
to
John David Jones
Lieutenant, United States Marine Corps …

If the bride or groom is enlisted, the branch of service is listed without the rank.

> Mr. and Mrs. Patrick Evans Smith
> request the honour of your presence
> at the marriage of their daughter
> Jane Ann
> to
> John David Jones
> United States Marine Corps ...

*Mr.* is never used to refer to an officer on active duty. If you're concerned about getting it right, contact a military chaplain on base or call your protocol officer for more direction.

## Final Military Wedding Thoughts

If you're getting married on a military base, let your guests know what, if any, forms of documentation they need to enter the base—a current driver's license and registration, for example. Include this on an insert with the invitation.

Your guests also need to know if they should allot extra time to make it past security at the base entrance and get to the chapel on time.

# Chapter 10

# Vacational Vows

## In This Chapter

- Planning a destination wedding
- The costs of destination weddings
- Playing tour guide to your wedding guests
- Parties after the fact

Some brides and grooms want to keep things simple, intimate, and unique. These folks know the way to keep stress levels down is to go on vacation—so why not get married there? In this chapter, I discuss the etiquette rules you need to know if you're planning a destination wedding. From the guest list to who pays for what, you have a lot of details to get right.

## Destination: Our Wedding!

Maggie met Alex later in life. Both had been married before, and both had grown children. They wanted to get married but couldn't imagine doing the whole traditional wedding thing. Their first vacation together had been to the Caribbean, and that's where they felt would be the best place to pledge their lives to each other. They kept the guest list small—just their children, their children's families, and a few close friends—and let their guests know months in advance about their plans.

The couple paid for their children's lodging and negotiated a discount rate for their friends at the same resort. They also set up a host of optional day trips and other ways for their guests to entertain themselves while there.

Maggie and Alex's wedding was a smashing success, not only by their account but by their families' as well. What Maggie and Alex did right was follow basic etiquette rules, including giving plenty of notice about their plans, and taking care of the small details so their guests merely had to show up and enjoy their time in such a tropical paradise.

## Check Your Calendar

Some brides and grooms choose destination weddings because they want the intimacy of having just the two of them there—a wedding and honeymoon all wrapped together. But others, like Maggie and Alex, envision their closest family members and friends joining them on their exotic journey. If it's important to you to have your parents or siblings or best friends with you, you should consult them before picking a date.

But don't open the entire calendar to your family and let them pick your wedding date. Select two or three dates that work best for you and ask those you're closest to which of those options works for them.

To increase your chances that close friends and family will be able to get the needed time off to travel to your destination wedding, choose holiday weekends such as Labor Day, Columbus Day, or Memorial Day. Most people already have these days off work and school then, so traveling is a bit easier.

### Bridal Blunder

Flights can be more expensive on holiday weekends, and some families use these weekends to make vacation plans of their own. So talk to your most important guests before deciding on a wedding date.

## The Guest List

The same rules apply about allowing guests to invite a date as with a traditional wedding. Although it might seem like you should allow every friend to invite a guest along, this is not the case. Only live-in significant others or those engaged have to be invited. But it is nice to allow your guests to travel with a companion, being that this will be a vacation for them as well as a wedding.

Also, unlike a regular wedding reception where you can invite only adults, it's not quite as easy when you're asking your guests to fly somewhere remote and take extra time off work. In these situations, you should include the children of adult guests on the invitation.

## Who Pays for What?

Destination weddings are perfect for people who don't want a lot of fuss but do want their closest loved ones present for their nuptials. The tricky part is figuring out who constitutes "closest loved ones."

The first thing you must do is figure out what expenses you're prepared to pay for and how much you have to spend. The bride and groom should pay for the following:

- Wedding reception (unless a parent or another loved one has offered to host)
- Rehearsal dinner
- Welcome party for guests upon everyone's arrival
- Morning-after brunch (may be hosted and paid for by someone else if they volunteer)
- Attendants' rooms (for at least two nights)

It's recommended that the bride and groom also pay for these:

- At least one group activity at the destination (a scuba-diving excursion or glass-bottom boat tour, for example)
- Transportation to and from the ceremony and reception sites
- Shuttle service from the airport to the hotel
- Travel expenses for attendants or loved ones who you really want there but can't afford to come

Attendants should pay for the following:

- Airfare or other travel expenses
- Formalwear and accessories
- Hair and makeup or other attendant-related activities
- Non-wedding-related meals and drinks
- Hotel accommodations if they're staying more than two nights

**Wedded Bliss**

You'll probably lean on your honor attendants more than ever to help you with last-minute wedding preparations, travel coordination, and on-site activities— but don't overburden them! Show your appreciation by giving them an extra-special gift of thanks, be it a gift certificate to use during their stay or something to pamper themselves with after they've returned home.

Guests should pay for these:

- Airfare or other travel expenses
- Hotel accommodations
- Non-wedding-related meals and drinks
- Any nonwedding activities they choose to do

Traditionally, the bride and groom (or parents, if someone is hosting the event) pick up the tab for at least two nights of lodging for any wedding attendants. But it's not necessary to have wedding attendants at all, especially at very small ceremonies. You really only need witnesses, and just about anyone can serve this purpose.

If your attendants are single and attending the wedding alone, it's okay for you to pair them up two to a room to save you some money. Be sure to let them know of such plans beforehand, so that if they'd like to "upgrade" to their own room they can pay the difference to do so. Any attendant who's bringing a spouse or significant other should be given his or her own room.

### History of Love

If you have your wedding and/or reception at a resort but not all your guests stay there, they might be charged a per-day fee for use of the facilities. You are obligated to pay for this fee.

Remember that even though you're asking potential wedding guests to spend lots of money on travel expenses, it's not necessary for you to foot the bill for their entertainment, apart from the wedding and reception.

When you have a budget set, you must research the destination you have in mind to find out how much this "low-key" wedding will set you back. Only then can you decide how many family members and friends you can comfortably afford to invite.

## Spreading the Word

For destination weddings, you need to mail save-the-date cards as far in advance as possible. Your guests need extra time to get extended time off work, make travel arrangements, and quite possibly alter their other vacation plans to save some money. Send the save-the-date cards 6 to 8 months before your nuptials, but never more than a year before your wedding date.

The cards should include the dates of your wedding getaway, all pertinent hotel or resort information, and any airline breaks you've researched that might be helpful. If there's room, include a little background on the destination you've selected; the dress code if you already know it; and any website links your guests might visit for more information on the resort, country, or town, or your own wedding website address if you have one.

### Wedded Bliss

If you and all your guests are staying at the same resort or hotel, negotiate as many perks as possible before you get there. Ask for reduced service charges on room rentals, reduced rates for excursions and rentals, and happy hour bar prices all day long. Also, see if they'll throw in a free hotel room or reduced-price suite for the bride and groom!

Invitations should go out earlier than you would send invitations for a regular wedding. Get them in the mail 10 to 12 weeks before the wedding, and ask to receive RSVPs no later than 6 weeks before the wedding. You'll need to confirm final head counts with your wedding coordinator at the destination around this time.

If you're worried that some people you'd like to invite won't be able to afford the trip, you should still invite them. Only inviting people who you're sure can make it is a sure way to hurt feelings and create resentment. For example, if you're keeping the guest list to immediate family, every sibling and their spouse should be invited.

If your RSVP date comes and goes and you still haven't heard from a handful of people, it's okay to call and ask them if they're coming.

## "We Got Married!"

If you're not having any type of reception back home, you can send out wedding announcements to family and close friends after you get married. These carry no obligation of sending a gift.

You may send formal announcements, as with this wording:

> Mr. and Mrs. Patrick Evans Smith
> are pleased to announce
> the marriage of their daughter
> Jane Ann
> to John David Jones

October tenth, two-thousand eight
Palma de Mallorca, Spain

Or you may send informal announcements that
might match the style of your wedding:

We tied the knot!
John and Jane Jones
October 10, 2008
Palma de Mallorca, Spain

If you're planning a reception back home sometime
after the wedding, invitations to that reception
should be worded carefully so people are not con-
fused about what they're being invited to. It's best
not to mention the wedding at all:

The pleasure of your company
is requested at the
wedding reception of
Mr. and Mrs. John and Jane Jones
Saturday, the eleventh of October
at 5 o'clock
Saratoga Spa Hotel
Saratoga Springs, New York

Some couples don't want guests to bring or send
gifts because of the added expense of the destination wedding, not to mention the fact that they
don't want to have to lug a bunch of gifts onto a
plane after their honeymoon. It's okay to request
by word of mouth that your guests not give you
gifts, but do not write this on the invitation.

## What to Wear

When it comes to destination wedding attire, etiquette rules are more relaxed than they are for formal weddings in traditional venues. If you're getting married on the beach, it's okay to go barefoot. It's okay to wear a floral dress instead of all white. This is your wedding, so dress as you want to.

When selecting your bride and groom wedding attire, keep the weather and ceremony site in mind. You want to look good against the backdrop you've chosen, so pick something that's appropriate for that location. Be sure you feel comfortable in whatever you choose, as it's sure to be a long, tiring day.

### Bridal Blunder

Don't risk losing your luggage—especially your wedding gown—on your wedding weekend! Carry the dress with you on the plane.

Be clear to your guests about how formal the attire will be for each of the planned events, from rehearsal dinner through any postwedding brunch. Keep your guests in mind when deciding on the dress code. If you're mixing the levels of formality between the various parties, your guests will have to pack that many more outfits, pairs of shoes, and handbags to match each occasion.

It isn't appropriate, however, to tell them exactly what they should wear. Although your vision of

everyone in white standing on the beach or everyone in floral Hawaiian prints may be perfect in
your mind, it seldom pans out that way in real life.
You run the risk of annoying your guests, who are
no doubt making quite an effort to attend. And
there's nothing more awkward than when one or
two guests show up in dark colors, ruining the
picture-perfect sea of white in your mind. You can't
make a particular style of dress mandatory.

# Playing Tour Guide

Sure, you're planning the wedding ceremony, reception, and rehearsal dinner. But your guests also will
be expecting you to at least point them in the direction of a few other things to do, see, and eat while
they're at your destination-wedding site. You don't
need to spend a lot of time playing tour guide, but
as host, you are responsible for giving them some
information they can use to plan their stay.

## Welcome!

Giving each couple a welcome bag of information
upon their arrival follows rules of good etiquette
and can save you from the headache of having
to give directions to a great eatery four different
times in one day. Here are a few helpful things to
include in a welcome bag:

- A note of welcome from the bride and
  groom.
- A detailed schedule of wedding-related festivities, including times, places, and dress code.

- A map of the area. Highlight the location of their hotel, any local restaurants you'd recommend, sightseeing hot spots, and your wedding site to help them get their bearings.

- Key contact information. This includes the cell phones and perhaps room numbers of any wedding attendants or family members you've selected as "go-to" people for the weekend. Don't include your hotel room number—unless you're prepared for some wedding night pranks!

- Sightseeing brochures, a list of local entertainment venues, and/or a local dining guide.

- Snacks or small gifts, preferably ones that match the destination or wedding theme (suntan lotion, a flip-flop key chain, locally grown fruit or other delicacy).

Every activity you plan should be optional, and nobody should be made to feel bad for opting out of the glass-bottom boat tour or windsurfing lesson. Everyone has a different idea about how they want to spend their vacation, so let the time away be just that: theirs.

Do think outside the box when it comes to offering activities. Just because you and your soon-to-be spouse are into physically challenging outings doesn't mean everyone you know will also want to go hang gliding. Have some alternative plans at the ready, such as historical tours and shopping excursions, for those with a milder wild side.

And keep in mind that too much of anything is never a good thing. Give your guests plenty of downtime to enjoy their vacations on their own, apart from your large group. Try to keep any planned activities to three hours or less each day.

## Who Pays for What?

Be careful of the way you word any invitation or enclosure that includes information about wedding-related (or not-so-related) excursions, meals, and activities. You don't want your guests assuming you're paying when you're not, or saving up all kinds of money thinking that they're paying, when in fact you've already taken care of the bill.

If you're paying for everyone to go on, say, a snorkeling excursion, invite them to this event in an enclosure along with your wedding invitation. If, however, you merely want to let them know of different activities that will be available, just mention that snorkeling will be available and give them any pertinent names, prices, and phone numbers so they can schedule their own excursion.

# Stateside Celebrations

When you decide to do a destination wedding, you're getting several things, including, quite possibly, a breathtaking backdrop to your wedding and a memorable vacation all rolled into one. You're also giving up a few things, including formal bridal showers and prewedding parties.

When it comes to eloping, people can feel hurt when they aren't included. It's hard for some family members to understand the reasoning behind your decision to keep your nuptials private or to celebrate them in an exotic location instead of at the local banquet hall. The best way to follow proper etiquette and avoid hurting people's feelings is to be up front with those you care about right from the start.

You might find that well-meaning family members still wish to throw you a bridal shower or host other prewedding parties. But be careful: wedding etiquette forbids people from being invited to a prewedding party who are not invited to the wedding.

## Prewedding Parties

Etiquette states that only people invited to a wedding should be invited to a shower. Because your destination wedding guest list is more than likely going to be quite small, so, too, should your bridal shower guest list.

This becomes tricky when you have well-meaning parents, siblings, and friends who still want to get in on all the hoopla of your wedding, even if they're not attending or not invited to the actual nuptials. Discourage them from inviting anyone who isn't invited to your wedding. But be prepared to compromise an etiquette rule in order to save someone's feelings from getting hurt.

## Postwedding Parties

It's okay to have a small group of friends and family accompany you to your destination wedding and then have a larger stateside reception. This can give the bride and groom the best of both worlds— an intimate wedding in a place they love *and* a chance to celebrate their nuptials with everyone they know.

Separate invitations should be sent to the wedding and the stateside celebration, even if you're inviting some or all of the same people. This rule doesn't apply in the smallest, most informal guest lists. In that case, one invitation probably will suffice.

You can have an elaborate, traditional wedding reception or a casual backyard barbecue. It's up to your style and your budget. It's okay to wear your wedding dress again and the groom may wear a tuxedo, although a simple suit is also appropriate. If you'd like to highlight your attendants, you may have them at the reception and give them a place of honor at the head table.

### Bridal Blunder

Be mindful of their budget when asking honor attendants to stand up with you at two different parties, especially if more travel and separate dresses are involved.

Gifts are not mandatory at a reception for a wedding that took place elsewhere. Many people still will bring gifts, but only those invited to the actual ceremony are expected to purchase wedding gifts.

People will be coming to see you and celebrate with you, but they also will be hoping to get a glimpse of what they missed at your faraway wedding. Be sure to have photos, a slideshow, or video of your nuptials to share with those who couldn't make it or weren't invited.

Chapter 11

# Once More, with Feeling

## In This Chapter

- Planning an encore wedding
- What to wear the second time around
- Vow renewal versus weddings
- Vow renewal and encore wedding gift-giving etiquette

Many people are re-marrying today. If the wedding you're planning isn't your first one, you probably have a whole host of questions regarding what you should wear, how elaborate a reception you should plan, and whom you should invite to this one.

In this chapter, I help you define what's proper when it comes to remarriage, from the dress code to the guest list.

## Encore Weddings

When Amber met Jordan, she knew he was her perfect mate and felt strongly that they would spend the rest of their lives together. But when

Jordan said he wanted a large, traditional wedding, Amber balked. She had been through a messy divorce just two years before and couldn't imagine sending invitations to so many people who had already sent her gifts and/or attended her wedding—to someone else.

Eventually Amber's sister convinced her that her loved ones were happy that she'd found someone so well suited for her and wanted to share in her celebration of this new love. Amber took her sister's advice, and she and Jordan plunged into wedding plans with abandon. The more they worked out the details, the more Amber came to realize that this was a totally new and different wedding—just as it would be a totally new and different marriage—and it deserved as much recognition and celebration as any other.

## What to Include This Time Around (and What to Omit)

It may be the second marriage for one or both of you, but it's the first marriage for you two as a couple. So you're free to include as many traditional wedding rituals as you like, from the father/daughter dance to a big fat wedding cake.

It's also acceptable to ask the same best man or maid of honor to stand up for you the second time around.

It's also okay not to include some of the traditional wedding elements like having attendants, holding a rehearsal dinner, having the bride escorted up the aisle, and doing a garter and bouquet toss. But do be mindful that if you're opting not to have attendants, you still need to have two witnesses sign the marriage license.

### Bridal Blunder

No matter how much you loved the reception hall or the ornate cathedral where you were first married, don't duplicate such venues the second time around or wear the same wedding dress.

## Spreading the News

When it comes to announcing your engagement, any children you have should be the first to know. Your parents should be informed next, followed by an ex-spouse if children are involved. The ex need not give his or her blessing for this new step you're taking, but they might be called on to help your children transition into this new life with you.

When a bride or groom is remarrying, sending wedding invitations can be stressful. Those remarrying think about how many of their invitees received a wedding invitation from them sometime in the past. But as long as the invitation is carefully and correctly worded, it should only bring to mind the happy occasion of your upcoming nuptials.

Here is suggested wording if the bride and groom are hosting the wedding.

Carolyn Leah Shultz
and
James Samuel Watson
invite you to share their joy
at their wedding
Saturday, the thirteenth of July
at five o'clock ...

When the bride and groom have children they
want mentioned in the invitation, use this wording:

Carolyn Leah Shultz
and
James Samuel Watson
together with their children
Beatrice Ann Shultz and
Lisa Marie Watson
request the honour of your presence
at their marriage ...

Here's another option for listing children on the
invitation:

Ms. Carolyn Leah Shultz
with her daughter Beatrice Ann Shultz
and
Mr. James Samuel Watson
with his daughter Lisa Marie
invite you to share their joy
in uniting these two families
Saturday, the thirteenth of July
at four o'clock ...

For weddings with 50 or fewer guests, you don't
need to send formal invitations. You can invite
people in person, on the phone, or by sending a
brief note through the mail.

It's perfectly acceptable to announce your marriage
in the newspaper as you would a first wedding. If
you're mailing wedding announcements, follow
the same rules and wording suggestions as for first
marriages.

### Bridal Blunder

Do not put wedding announcements
in the mail until the wedding day or
afterward.

## VIPs and Invitees

Those planning encore weddings also pore over
their guest list, searching for possible etiquette
missteps or something that might cause hurt feelings or awkward moments. In general, you may
invite anyone you wish to your wedding, including
friends and family who attended your first.

However, unless your ex-spouse is a close friend
and also is friendly with your current love, the
ex should not be invited to the wedding. Inviting
former in-laws also is a judgment call you should
make based on your current relationship and your
soon-to-be-spouse's feelings on the subject.

Even if you're paying for the wedding, it's customary for you to ask both sets of parents if they have any close friends they'd like to invite. Chances are, an encore wedding will include more of your friends than your parents' friends, so adding a few to the guest list to please your folks shouldn't be a problem. You needn't follow the 30-30-40 rule outlined in Chapter 1 unless it's a large, traditional wedding with all the trimmings—or if they are hosting the party.

## All Dressed in ... White?

One of the biggest wedding etiquette myths is that it's not appropriate for second-time brides to wear white on their wedding day. This isn't outdated; it's simply not true. A bride may wear any color or style of dress that flatters her. Another myth is that second-time brides should wear a shorter dress and avoid anything ankle-length. That, too, is false. A bride should wear a dress that suits her wedding and her style.

However, second-time brides should forgo a blusher veil that covers the face; this is a traditional style reserved for first-time brides. You can wear a veil that cascades down the back, if it suits the style and formality of your dress and wedding. Also, trains are fine, but a simple one is better suited than cathedral length.

If you're having a traditional ceremony with attendants, all the usual etiquette rules apply. The style of formalwear should coordinate with the formality of the event you're planning. It's ultimately up to you what you have your attendants (and any children who are in the wedding) wear, but it's a good idea to consult with them about their tastes and give them options whenever possible.

## Exchanging Vows

If you used traditional wedding vows in your first ceremony, it is advisable that you write your own vows or together select the wording for your vows this time around.

## Blending Families

Remarriages often aren't just about joining two people; they're about joining two families. You can include children in a remarriage ceremony by having them in the wedding party. A child can stand up next to his or her parent as an honor attendant or be a junior bridesmaid, junior groomsmen, ring bearer, or flower girl. Or a child may escort his or her mother up the aisle and then take a seat of honor in the front pew.

Be mindful of age guidelines for attendants. For example, it's not appropriate to make the groom's 11-year-old daughter the flower girl in his wedding. She's too old for this role. Instead, she could serve as a junior bridesmaid.

You can also include your children in your wedding by mentioning them in your vows. This is a good way to show them that you are pledging your commitment to the entire family, not just their parent.

Here's an example of a wedding vow that includes a child from a previous marriage:

> I, Aubrey, take you, Scott, to be my husband.
> I promise to love and honor you all the days
> of my life with all that I have and all that I
> am. I enter this marriage with my eyes and
> my heart wide open, anxious to share your
> dreams and ease your fears. I will strive to be
> not only a loving wife but a close and trusted
> friend and guardian to Ben, whom I love and
> cherish as my own child. You are the two
> most important men in my life, and I will
> love you both, always.

If you'd like to include the children in the ceremony but want to use a more traditional wedding vow, you can recite a separate vow (pledged after you and your spouse exchange vows) to the children, as Cliff and Angela did. They centered their vows on their promises of support and fidelity to each other and then offered a special vow to their children:

> Lily and Tommy, we promise to be faithful
> to your needs, to support and care for you
> in good times and in bad, in sickness and in
> health. We will love you and laugh with you,
> play with you, and pray for you. We know
> that a happy family is one that knows how to
> compromise, and we will do that. But we will
> never compromise our love for you.

Still another appropriate way to blend two families during a wedding ceremony is to light a unity candle or give each child a family medallion that signifies their new union.

## Showers of Love

Any wedding comes with lots of well-wishing and often more than one pre- or postwedding party. If this is your second (or third) time around this particular block, you might want to scale down the number of parties given in your honor.

A giftless shower might be a good option if you're concerned about making people who've given you shower and wedding gifts before feel like they should do so again. It's okay to include a note about the shower being "giftless" on the shower invitation, although you would never do this on a wedding invitation.

Couples showers and themed showers often work very well for encore wedding brides. Here are some themes that work well for encore wedding showers:

- Garden party shower, with gifts such as gardening tools, patio accessories, and garden art
- Night on the town shower, with tickets to local theater productions, movie houses, or restaurants
- Wine cellar shower, with fine wine, wine accoutrements, and stemware gifts

A note about hosting: just as parents or siblings should not host a shower for a bride, so should her own children not play host at a bridal shower for her. It's customary for her close friends to do the shower hosting duties.

## Gift-Giving Do's and Don'ts

Those getting married for the second (or third or fourth …) time can still register for gifts. A gift registry may be mentioned in a shower invitation, but be aware that guests who attended your first wedding and gave you a gift are not obligated to give another gift this time around—for either the shower or the wedding.

It's still appropriate to give thank you gifts to people in your wedding party (if you have one). It's also a nice gesture for either spouse to give a gift, something small and meaningful, to their new stepchild. This will go a long way in building a happy blended family.

# Vow Renewals

Some couples like to celebrate an anniversary milestone like 25 years together by having a vow renewal. Others rush through the initial wedding process due to military or other reasons, and later wish to have more family and friends help them celebrate their marriage.

The most important thing to understand about vow renewals is that they are not second weddings.

You cannot get married in a quickie ceremony at city hall and then get married again in a big church with all your loved ones there. That second, church service would be a vow renewal, and it comes with it a separate set of etiquette guidelines.

## Vow Renewal Etiquette

The husband and wife are typically the host at a vow renewal, not Mom and Dad. Keep this in mind when deciding what you can afford to spend. Occasionally, a couple's grown children plan and host the event. This is perfectly acceptable, and the host(s) should be made clear on the invitation.

A few traditional wedding elements have no place in a vow-renewal ceremony and reception:

- The bride being "given away" by her father or another father figure. A charming alternative to this is for the couple to walk up the aisle together, or for her children to escort her up the aisle.

- Traditional procession before the ceremony.

- Father/daughter dance.

- Wedding cake. Cake may be served, but it should look different from a traditional wedding cake. Writing on the cake is acceptable, making it more of a "Congratulations!" or anniversary cake.

- Garter and bouquet toss.

- Best man toast. There is no best man toast because there is no best man. The wife already married her best man—her husband.

## Spreading the News

Vow renewal invitations should be as formal as the ceremony itself. As with a regular wedding invitation, whoever hosts the event, whether it's the married couple or their children, should be listed as such on the invitation. Here are some suggested wordings:

> The honour of your presence is requested
> at the renewal of wedding vows of
> Mr. and Mrs. Daniel Robert Anderson
> Sunday, the first of September
> at three o'clock
> First Baptist Church
> Memphis, Tennessee

> Andrew Joseph and Allison Grace
> invite you to share in our joy
> as our parents
> Mr. and Mrs. Daniel Robert Anderson
> renew their vows
> Sunday, the first of September
> at three o'clock
> First Baptist Church

> The children of
> Amy and Daniel Anderson
> request the honour of your presence
> at the reaffirmation ceremony
> of their parents …

Writing "No gifts, please" on a wedding invitation is not acceptable, as you know, but because this is not a wedding, it's fine to do so on your vow renewal invitation. However, you most likely will receive some gifts, especially if your vow renewal coincides with an anniversary, so be gracious about receiving gifts, and send a thank you note promptly after the event.

## VIPs and Invitees

The point of having honor attendants at a wedding is to have the witnesses required to validate the marriage license. So a vow renewal obviously doesn't have a need for honor attendants. It's okay to invite your original honor attendants, but there's no need to have anyone standing beside you at the altar besides your spouse.

However, if you're re-creating your original wedding, it's okay to ask your honor attendants to be a part of the ceremony this time around, too. They would not wear formalwear or bridesmaid dresses, but would opt for a suit or shorter, less formal dress that matches the formality of the occasion.

## All Dressed in ... White?

Unless you are re-creating your original wedding day by wearing your original wedding dress (and good for you if it still fits!), you should not wear a wedding dress to a vow renewal. This is a reaffirmation of your vows, not the real thing.

Fancy cocktail dresses or evening dresses that match the formality of the event are preferred. And keep in mind that vow renewals are typically less formal than weddings. You can, however, wear white to your vow renewal.

## Exchanging Vows

A renewal of your wedding vows needn't be the two of you re-reciting the vows you pledged the first time around, although that is a perfectly acceptable, sentimental way to go. You may write new vows that speak to how your relationship has evolved and where it's headed. Or check with the officiant presiding over the service, as he or she might have a specifically worded ceremony that's used for vow renewals in that venue.

## Showers of Love

Bridal showers and bachelor and bachelorette parties are traditions meant for single women and men, not those who've already been married. Bachelor parties signify the last night out as a single man, so if you're renewing your vows, that ship sailed long ago and is not appropriate to hop aboard once again.

If you're re-creating your original wedding day for your vow renewal, it's okay for the women close to you to hold a shower in your honor, but you shouldn't register for gifts.

# Index